THE NATURE OF EXISTENCE

i

THE NATURE OF EXISTENCE

HEALTH, WELLBEING AND THE NATURAL WORLD

CHARLOTTE HARKNESS

First published 2019 by
RED GLOBE PRESS

Red Globe Press in the UK is an imprint of Springer Nature Limited, registered in England, company number 785998, of 4 Crinan Street, London, N1 9XW.

Red Globe Press® is a registered trademark in the United States, the United Kingdom, Europe and other countries.

ISBN 978–1–137–57686–6

This book is printed on paper suitable for recycling and made from fully managed and sustained forest sources. Logging, pulping and manufacturing processes are expected to conform to the environmental regulations of the country of origin.

A catalogue record for this book is available from the British Library.

A catalog record for this book is available from the Library of Congress.

CONTENTS

LIST OF FIGURES

LIST OF EXERCISES

ACKNOWLEDGMENTS

The origins of this book began during my doctoral studies at New School of Psychotherapy and Counselling (NSPC), though my interest and inspiration in my relationship with nature goes back as far as I can remember. I am forever grateful to my parents and grandparents for a childhood spent in beautiful places, many of them cold and rugged, but beautiful to me nonetheless. My peers at NSPC encouraged me to follow my passion during research seminars and helped me to move away from the certainty of intellectual knowledge towards focusing on an area that initially did not seem to make much sense to me, but that I felt drawn to in a much more holistic way.

My supervisors for my doctoral research 'An Existential Formulation of Transformative Experiences in Nature' were Rosemary Lodge and Emmy van Deurzen. Rosemary and Emmy were pivotal in encouraging me to move down this path and in valuing staying with experience. Rosemary immersed herself in my work and renewed my passion when I hit inevitable stumbling blocks. Her exemplary standards continue to inspire me. Huge thanks go to the generous research participants who gave their time to meet with me and talk about their powerful experiences in being in nature and to Emma Wilkinson for being alongside me throughout this journey. Thanks also to the team at Red Globe Press, in particular Peter Hooper and Hannah Watson.

The doctoral research on which this book is based was concluded at a very difficult time in my life and my final thesis was submitted the day after my first husband, Ian Macgregor, was diagnosed with incurable cancer. Ian's interest in the outdoors and his support for my work was pivotal in my journey to becoming a psychotherapist, researcher and writer in this area.

Throughout his illness and after his death I was Deputy Course Leader of the DProf at NSPC and Emmy van Deurzen, Digby Tantam, Rosemary Lodge, Dawn Farrow, Chloe Paidoussis-Mitchell, Sasha Smith and the rest of the NSPC team resolutely encouraged me to continue with my work and my passion, supporting me in the midst of emotional pain and chaos.

My children, Josephine, Tristan, Kerys and Lily were aged between 14 and 4 years old when I started my doctoral studies and I am proud of and very grateful for their love, enthusiasm and resilience. My walking partners over the years, Austin and Laura Heraty, Ellie and Tom Vandyk and Nick Peek have all, in very different ways, supported and sustained me and given me insights into their own diverse relationships with the natural world.

In January 2015, when I was least expecting it and when I was beginning to emerge from the darkest of times, I met James Harkness and my life quite simply, and rather wonderfully, was thrown on its head. Eighteen months after we met we married and we spent a gorgeous honeymoon touring in California. Standing in the majesty of Yosemite National Park and looking out across the raw beauty of the west coast of the States to the ocean took my inspiration with the natural world to a different, more spiritual plane. Sharing such powerful beauty surrounded by love revitalized my impetus to complete the writing of this book. Thank you James for your love and laughter, for everything.

1

Introduction

To consider our relationship with nature in the context of our mental and emotional wellbeing seems outside of the norm of much of counselling and psychotherapy theory and practice; the preserve of the eco-psychology and eco-psychotherapy approaches. Yet there is a marked difference between these approaches, which have nevertheless inspired me enormously, and my humble musings in this book. While my own environmental concerns continue to solidify and my affinity with the philosophy that underlies much of the eco-writing is strong, I am not in any sense endeavouring to espouse an environmental approach in this book or to explain or educate the reader in the practicalities or intricacies of eco-therapy or eco-psychology: writers such as Buzzell and Chalquist (2009), Jordan (2014) and Jordan and Hinds (2016) focus on the theory and practice of specific outdoor and nature-based practices and offer guidance on central aspects and related issues of taking therapy outdoors. Rather than focusing on eco-therapy or following a specific environmental approach, my aim is really a much simpler one: to shine a light on the potential benefits of giving some attention to nature in our quest for emotional and mental health and wellbeing. We talk about 'human nature' in everyday speak, and from that we might assume that the connection between nature and our emotional and mental wellbeing might be an easy idea to work with. Yet, when I first began to explore the subject of our wellbeing in relation to the natural world as part of my professional doctoral studies in existential psychotherapy and I tentatively talked about my subject to my peers there was a general somewhat bemused, quizzical response. This rather increased my resolve. The mental and emotional benefits of nature and the great outdoors have begun to be taken seriously over the last decade, outside of the niche areas of wilderness therapy and adventure therapy and the eco-therapy and eco-psychology arenas. The benefits of green exercise were noted by Mind (2007) and architects and urban designers increasingly endeavour to incorporate nature and green space into buildings and urban areas in order to improve the quality of our daily lives.

This book sets off from the premise that our being in nature matters and throughout it attempts to challenge various ideas of separation or splitting off of head from body and human being from world. Our English language at times tests us, in that it leads us towards a more individualistic frame. Even the language of the collective, 'we', 'us' and 'they', contains the assumption of multiple individual separated beings. Existential philosophers and psychotherapists have endeavoured to address this, as we will see in Chapter 2.

The natural world, and human existence within it, is of a scale that means that it would be an impossible feat to do more than scrape the surface of our intricate, beautiful relationship with nature. The key ideas that are considered in the following chapters are inspired by my reading, research and study for this project and, most importantly, by the voices of the research participants that spoke to me about their powerful, transformative experiences in nature (Macgregor 2013). My doctoral research was conceived from my personal relationship with nature and inspired both by a lifetime living in and exploring beautiful natural environments that really touched me and by some particularly transformative experiences that I will draw on throughout this book. Although my research was heuristic, I interviewed a range of research participants about a diverse variety of transformative experiences that they had experienced in nature. All of my research participants described the impact of these experiences on their wider lives and, in particular, the enduring impact that they had. The key ideas in this book are underpinned by the existential psychotherapeutic four-dimensional model of living, as outlined by Deurzen and Arnold-Baker (2005). Viewing existence through the sphere of the four dimensions: the physical, social, spiritual and personal, already begins the process of rebalancing how we see issues with living, moving us away from the more individualist views of our present Western age (Deurzen 2012). Chapter 2 places the human–nature relationship in the context of these more usual views of human existence, and encourages a suspension of ideas about our relationship with nature that tend to assume distinct splits between us and the natural world. Twenty-first century views of mental health and wellbeing, such as those outlined by the American Psychiatric Association (APA) in the Diagnostic and Statistical Manual of Mental Disorders V (DSM V) (American Psychiatric Association (APA) 2013), pay little heed to the context of distress or wellbeing outside of the confines of our minds and heads, and the focus is almost exclusively at an individual level, rather than on the relationship or on interconnection. An existential approach to living, in contrast, situates the human firmly in relationship in the world and therefore provides a philosophical backdrop that makes exploring our being in nature a much more understandable endeavour than if we were stepping off on this journey from the vantage of a more isolationist approach. Having said that, it is my aim in this writing that a detailed understanding of existential philosophy and psychotherapy is not a requirement for following the key themes and ideas; rather, all that is needed is an open mind and curiosity to see the rich potential that exists as part of our being in nature.

My primary wish in writing this text is to facilitate readers to bring what we usually see as the 'outside' into both therapeutic ways of working and into day-to-day living. This is not about being outside more though, or about a concerted effort towards a more environmental stance (though I would not discourage either). It is rather that I hope readers will be encouraged to challenge the deeply engrained views about what health is and the entrenched assumptions about where the locus for healing might be situated that reside in much of our routines and practices. Chapter 3 focuses on the rhythms of existence and provides an opportunity to question our relationship with time and history. What happens when we are thrown off kilter from our bodily rhythms or lose touch with seasonality, disconnected from our natural rhythms? How does holding on to fixed ideas of self and personality, who we are, limit our potential and how might nature show us an alternative? Chapter 4 focuses on our relationship with our physical selves and provides a critique of the routine objectification and manipulation of our bodies. If we are not able to feel at home in our bodies how on earth are we to begin to feel at home in our wider physical environments? What are the implications for feeling disembodied and what does our disconnection from our physical world mean for our health and wellbeing? How does our routine objectification of ourselves impact on how we do or do not nourish and sustain ourselves? What is the difference between living on our planet, rather than in it? These themes pave the way for Chapter 5, where we discuss the nature of healing. From a position of understanding that people have turned to nature for healing for centuries it is perhaps more appropriate to consider when we ceased looking outside of the boundaries of our own skin for health and healing. As well as looking at specific practices of healing in nature, metaphors from nature are used as a guide towards reframing how we approach personal dilemmas. Particular themes in this chapter include looking at loss, bereavement and grief.

Ideas of identity and self are explored in Chapter 6, where we raise the question 'Who am I?'. The boundary, if there is such a thing, between self and the natural world has been raised as an issue for discussion in earlier chapters, and in this chapter we will explore it further and look at its relevance in terms of how we understand our selves, particularly in the context of being of being an integral part in a much wider whole. Chapter 7 examines peak experiences, particularly those of a transformative quality, and reflects on what might happen when we thwart the potential for nature to take us out of the ordinary and the everyday. Ideas relating to self-harm and addiction are considered.

Of course, we are all alive *in* nature, as we sit inhaling and exhaling and go about our everyday lives. It is not just the particular sort of nature that we live our daily lives in that matters, though of course it does matter a great deal. What is really at the heart of this writing is the need to think about the space, time and intent that we give to our *being as part of that nature* and to explore as creatively as possible the rich potential that we have before us. The ideas that follow in these pages might at first glance fall outside of what we more usually and comfortably consider to be the realm of health and wellbeing. I hope that they pique your curiosity and enthusiasm.

I watch as the wind rolls across the garden and booms against the brick-work of my room. I watch the sycamore trees reflected in the mirror by my desk. The booming intensifies; the sycamores are dancing. Love moves inside me, and it seems – even mediated by a mirror that my love is recip-rocated. It has been like that as long as I remember, and really, there's nothing to be said about it. I love Earth; it feels that Earth loves me: that's just how it is...

Perraton Mountford (2006, p. 99)

2

The Context of the Human–Nature Relationship

We are born into nature, we live our lives as part of nature and we finally die into the natural world. The natural world is the context and sustenance of our life. In this chapter, we will situate our existence in the natural world in relation to the theory and practice of mainstream psychology, psychotherapy and medicine and more widely in noted works of literature and the arts. This chapter will begin to explore how the human–nature relationship has been viewed historically from religious perspectives and also through the traditions of indigenous populations. We will compare and contrast this with a twenty-first century Western conceptualization of this most important of relationships. The works of key eco-psychologists and eco-therapists will be introduced, including Hillman (1995), Harper (1995) and Buzzell and Chalquist (2009), and there will be a focus on how these writers approach nature and our existence. It will outline the four dimensions of existence: the physical, social, personal and spiritual dimensions as proposed in the writings of leading existential philosopher and psychotherapist Emmy van Deurzen (2012). The ideas of other notable existential philosophers and practitioners who also focus on a more holistic view of existence will be explored, including Heidegger (1962), Milton (2010), Merleau-Ponty (1962) and Sartre (1946). Their writings will be contrasted with more dualistic, split ways of approaching our being in the world, particularly the sorts of views that underpin our present-day health and social care service construction and provision. Key themes that will be explored include disconnection, nature and healing, potential transformative experiences, spiritual journeys, view of self and present-day mental illness conceptualizations.

Disconnection and connection

> No man is an island, entire of itself; every man is a piece of the continent, a part of the main. If a clod be washed away by the sea, Europe is the less, as well as if a promontory were, as well as if a manor of thy friend's or of thine own were: any man's death diminishes me, because I am involved in mankind, and therefore never send to know for whom the bells tolls; it tolls for thee.
>
> John Donne, Meditation XVII (2012, p. 46)

John Donne's beautifully evocative description of connection and relationship between humans and between us and nature jars rather sharply with twenty-first century ideas of how we are conditioned to view ourselves and our being. Our modern discourse around self and personality focuses on defining our existence in isolated, separatist and absolute terms. Even our language – I, You, They – rests on an underlying premise of separation. The notion that we each stand as individual, firmly boundaried and independent entities is everywhere, not least in the realms of mainstream psychiatry and psychology, and in health services more generally. We are categorized as either 'normal' or 'disordered' on an entirely independent basis, regardless of our environmental contexts, or our relationships, or our experiences in the worlds in which we live. We are firmly whisked away from any context and our wellbeing is rarely considered through a relational lens as part of each 'other'. Any kind of environmental or situational slant is largely dismissed.

Individualist ethos

Carl Jung, the Swiss psychiatrist and psychotherapist and widely acknowledged father of analytic psychology, wrote of the separatist, individualist ethos of the twentieth century 'I remain I and you remain you' (Jung 1975, p. 586). This individualistic ethos is familiar to any person who has had any kind of encounter with the mainstream psychiatric system's approach to diagnosing all sorts of mental or emotional problems with living, as outlined in the Diagnostic and Statistical Manual V (DSM V) (American Psychiatric Association (APA) 2013). DSM V barely acknowledges any inter-human impact on health, distress, wellbeing and healing, let alone any connection with nature or the physical environment (American Psychiatric Association (APA) 2013). As a species, us human beings have positioned ourselves firmly at the top of the evolutionary tree, with each small step on the branches feeling increasingly distanced from the soil of its roots. The vast range of technological advancements of the last century that continue into this one increases our distance from the earth and from our physical roots, meaning that we are less likely than ever to shine a light on our relationship with nature, to attend to it either for our individual or reciprocal wellbeing.

Paul Maiteny, a psychotherapist, anthropologist and ecologist, notes that although it is actually impossible for us to not be part of the whole, we 'use the evolutionary gifts of our mind, consciousness, free will, intellect, imaginations, to insist on behaving as if we are not' (Maiteny 2012, p. 57). It is a very particular kind of denial attitude or state that we have found ourselves in and that we continue to perpetuate. While Maiteny's writing here is primarily focused on the context of considering approaches to what he considers the extreme environmental crisis of our times, his thoughts and ideas could equally be describing the mainstream approach to health, wellbeing and psychotherapy – indeed to living in general. We behave and view ourselves and each other largely in a vacuum. Stevens (2010) notes that while general healthcare service provision has at least begun to appreciate that mind and body cannot be completely extracted from each other, the awareness that 'the separation of self and environment is an equally false dichotomy' has not yet been widely recognized outside of the narrow restraints of the eco-therapy, eco-psychology and environmental psychology arenas (Stevens 2010, p. 265).

A more normal, day-to-day view of our existence in nature is perhaps that it is better for us to have some green outdoor time and space, that nature is restorative; and it is fairly widely documented across a range of more popular literature and in the press that when people are out in nature, spending time walking, for example, or in environmental restoration projects or wilderness retreats they feel broadly better about themselves. Although this is almost viewed as a given, little credence is really afforded to the relationship when we find ourselves confronting head-on issues relating to our mental health and emotional wellbeing. To some extent this normal view is just accepted and left dormant, rather than any concerted effort being made to grapple with, unravel and understand what we might be talking about. In some measure, our language does not help in encouraging enquiry into our being in nature, in that polarities and the construction of difference are all-pervasive and assumed.

The nature of existential being

In contrast to the vast majority of the mainstream psychiatric and psychological attitudes, existential philosophy and existential approaches to psychotherapy and counselling psychology view human beings not as isolated static personalities, but rather as relational existents *in-the-world* (Deurzen 2012). An existential understanding of what it means to be a human being holds at its centre the social, cultural and physical dimensions in which a person exists (Deurzen 2012). From both a biological and psychological perspective 'we exist in the world and our interdependence is total' (Milton 2010, p. 294). Martin Heidegger used the term 'Dasein', translated into 'being-in-the-world', to attempt to show this interconnection (Heidegger 1962). The term Dasein demonstrates how Heidegger opposed viewing a person in isolation from being in relationship, opposed the extraction of person from world and acknowledged and put at the centre the totally interconnected basis of living and being (Heidegger 1962). In his essay on existence and humanism, Jean-Paul Sartre asks 'What do we mean by saying that existence precedes essence? We mean that man first of all exists, encounters himself, surges up in the world – and defines himself afterwards' (Sartre 1946, p. 29). From Sartre's account, the self that I define, the 'I' that I speak of, arises out of my being in the world, rather than as a predefined,

firmly boundaried personality entity implanted onto an already existing world. Heidegger's writing proposes that the 'compound expression
of "Being-in-the-World" indicates in the very way we have coined it,
that it stands for a unitary phenomenon. This primary datum must be
seen as a whole' (Heidegger 1962, p. 78). Heidegger's account of the
relationship between natural world and human existence attempts to
do away with the conception of separately defined entities, placing
'world' as integral to any awareness of being 'Being-in-the-world shall
first be made visible with regard to that item of its structure which is
the "world" itself' (Heidegger 1962, p. 91).

Both Heidegger and Sartre give voice and prominence not just to
relationship, but to unitary existence – that we are *one in* and with
the world, which goes much further than individuals relating to each
other in a particular context. Maurice Merleau-Ponty (1969) describes
the intrinsic human–nature existence outside of the usual subject–
object split, concentrating on the middle ground of phenomenology. His eco-phenomenological approach focuses on the relational,
whether the beings that are part of the relationship are human or
otherwise (Merleau-Ponty 1969). An eco-phenomenological approach
is concerned with the material quality of being in relation (Brown
and Toadvine 2003). Abram (1996) refers to the 'animate earth' and
focuses on our being part of the animate earth in which we experience (Brown and Toadvine 2003, p. x).

Contemporary existential psychotherapy theorists also focus on
relational lived experience (Cooper 2003; Deurzen 2012; Spinelli
2007). Emmy van Deurzen's four-dimensional model considers the
individual's relational existence on the physical dimension as well as
the personal, social and spiritual dimensions (Deurzen 2012). Deurzen
and Arnold-Baker together write about how the 'material world is the
foundation of any person's existence' (Deurzen and Arnold-Baker 2005,
p. 30). Our relationship with the world that we live in is important to
us: how we relate to our natural environment, our own physical sensory experiences, the qualities of the world around us. An existential
phenomenological approach to therapy practice focuses firmly on the
inter-relatedness of our being (Deurzen 2012). However, even from
an existential perspective which focuses considerably more on inter-
relatedness or lived experience in context, the relational focus is still

considered primarily from the standpoint of the human–human sphere, rather than a broader human–nature relationship. While existential approaches to psychotherapy and counselling psychology do explore and value experiencing on the physical dimension of existence and acknowledge this as important in therapeutic practice, there remains something of a hierarchy or separation of *place* in the dimensional structure, and of *place* within the physical dimension in particular. Place is assumed to be *the location of* an experience, rather than integral to understanding life or to the understandings of experiences that might be described as residing on more social, personal or spiritual planes. Place remains the backdrop to experience, rather like a stage on which actors act, rather than a dynamic, integral part of the performance of living, of being in the world.

While an existential approach to psychotherapeutic practice gives some credence to interconnection and our being in nature, a person-centred perspective, as the name suggests, tends to focus on the individual in less of an interconnected, relational way than in existential philosophy (Rogers 1951). Carl Rogers, the father of person-centred therapy, proposes that 'Every individual exists in a continually changing world of experience of which he is the center' (Rogers 1951, p. 483). Although the boundaries between 'self' and 'world' seem more demarcated in Rogers's writings, he does go on to later describe how 'the actualising tendency of individual organisms is a microcosm of a broader "formative" tendency that is evident in cells, galaxies etc. This creates potential for human beings to develop an ever deeper awareness of their place in the universe, and can serve as a basis for a theory of humanistic psychology' (Rogers 1978, p. 46).

Rogers describes how we share something, some sort of tendency or attribute, with our wider world. Rogers's writing resonates with Sartre's thoughts on the experience of being outside of oneself; that 'it is in projecting and losing himself beyond himself that he makes man to exist; and, on the other hand, it is by pursuing transcendent aims that he himself is able to exist' (Sartre 1946, p. 67). The boundary between self and other, whether other is person, nature or world, is not completely clear cut; it is, at the very least, more porous than the mainstream individualist discourse around 'self' of our present age.

With such relational, world-based underpinnings to the writings of both existential philosophers and therapists, it is surprising to find such limited description of transformative experiences in nature. While Deurzen and Milton have provided accounts (Deurzen 2008; Milton 2008) these are by no means representative or extensive descriptions, though they do offer the sort of invitation to further exploration that to some extent fuelled my original research on transformative experiences in nature and, indeed, this writing endeavour.

The eco-writers: healing the earth, healing the mind

Once we start to approach the boundaries of self with a little more fluidity, we begin to open ourselves up to the possibility of being touched by the other and we are able to move into the realms of the eco-psychology and eco-therapy writers and practitioners. We can start to more creatively and naively imagine how we interconnect with our world, how we might relate to nature and consider the natural world and place in relation to our mental health and wellbeing. James Hillman (1995), an eco-psychologist and neo-Jungian writing in the foreword of Roszak's *Ecopsychology: Restoring the Earth, Healing the Mind* (Roszak et al. 1995) says 'There is only one core issue for all psychology. *Where is the "me"*? Where does the "me" begin? Where does the "me" stop. Where does the "other" begin?' (Hillman 1995, p. xxvii). Hillman describes how 'for most of history, psychology took for granted an intentional subject: the biographical "me" that was the agent and the sufferer of all "doings"' (Hillman 1995, p. xxvii).

Hillman suggests that 'the deepest self cannot be confined to "in here" because we can't be sure it is not also or even entirely "out there"' (Hillman 1995, p. xix). Existential writers, such as Merleau-Ponty, have highlighted the holistic nature of our experience, pointing towards the somewhat arbitrary distinction made between 'self' and 'not-self': 'Our own body is in the world as the heart is in the organism: it keeps the visible spectacle alive, it breathes life into it and sustains it inwardly, and with it forms a system' (Merleau-Ponty 1962, p. 371).

The border between self and the natural world is therefore considered a more subjective cut within one system, rather than demarcating two different systems: 'we can make it at the skin or we can take it as far out as we like – to the deep oceans and distant stars' (Hillman 1995, p. xix). As Roszak suggests, the critical point is not so much where we decide that the boundary is; rather what is more important and significant is 'the recognition of uncertainty about making the cut at all' (Roszak et al. 1995, p. xix). From Roszak's perspective, it is not necessary to view our existence in isolationist, separatist terms. Metzner writes about 'green psychology' from the stance of wanting to change and transform our relationship with the earth in which we live, suggesting that 'seeing ourselves as communicating nerve cells in the body of Gaia, Earth, necessitates a shift in perspective' (Metzner 1999, p. 37). From this perspective, we are not on earth, nor are *we* in *it*: we are cells forming part of the whole. From this vantage, then, the potential for change and transformation in any part of the system, so for example, my wellbeing or your mental health, might rest anywhere within the whole system. Metzner suggests that we do not have to look for solutions or ideas solely within the specific, arbitrary frame (or cell) in which a problem or dilemma might arise (Metzner 1999).

In a similar vein, Bateson (1972) also takes a more systemic and holistic focus, proposing that to consider our existence as ending at the skin of our bodies is to deny the presence of a whole and to have an incomplete perspective. Bateson questions the notion of 'I', the location of boundaries of self and the extent to which we, as humans, tend to speak from an 'I' viewpoint. Bateson considers that how we conceptualize self within the holistic system influences our relationship with self and the system, influences the whole (Bateson 1972; Rust and Totton 2012). Bateson cites the seminal writings of Martin Buber and his description of the I–Thou and I–It relationships, where the more usual day-to-day pattern of relating to the world is in the I–It mode, as separate human to inanimate object (Buber 1937). Bateson suggests that an 'I–Thou relationship is conceivable between man and his society or ecosystem' (Bateson 1972, p. 452). This approach to relationship, where love, care and a fluid attitude to potential experience are privileged over purpose and function, lays the groundwork for a much deeper emotional experience within nature, a relationship that falls outside of a more separatist, exclusively human-centric ethos. Bodnar, a relational psychoanalyst, has researched the transformed relationship between human and their ecosystems with the 'assumption that the human relationship to the physical environment was another object relationship' (Bodnar 2012, p. 17). Bodnar noted that the people that 'conceive nature as a component of the self have changed the way they live' and in particular they have what are described as 'deeper more complex relationships to the ecosystems' (Bodnar 2012, p. 27). How we conceptualize self and nature, therefore, would seem to have an impact on how we relate in it and how we experience ourselves. The writers described here believe passionately in the deep connection between a hurting earth and a hurting mind, and as the title of Roszak's book suggests: *Ecopsychology: Restoring the Earth Healing the Mind*, that healing both are intrinsically connected (Roszak et al. 1995).

Martin Jordan suggested that we have developed a split and separation between nature and human being in order to try and provide a safeguard for ourselves, attempting to distance us from our vulnerabilities and the reality of our actual inter-dependency with our planet and the environment (Jordan 2009b). It is tempting to see the writings of the eco-therapists and eco-psychologists as new and somewhat alternative. However, the relationship between man and environment, looking to the earth and environment for healing, guidance and sustenance, is firmly embedded in both ancient and modern indigenous and tribal cultures and rituals and throughout literature (Greenwood and Leeuw 2007; Higley and Milton 2008; Roszak et al. 1995). As an example, Emerson's beautiful words from 1849, 'In the wilderness, I find something more dear and connate than in streets or villages. In the tranquil landscape, and especially in the distant line of the horizon, man beholds somewhat as beautiful as his own nature' (Emerson 1849, p. 4).

Although an existential approach does allow for our being embodied in the natural world in its philosophy, largely the relationship with our physical context is ignored when we consider mental health and emotional wellbeing. Higley and Milton suggest that our being in nature is 'a neglected relationship in counselling psychology' and they consider that this might be an important part of some of our present-day problems and distress (Higley and Milton 2008, p. 10). Implicit in this statement is the reverse of the argument; that focusing on our relationship with nature might be at least part of a resolution of some of these concerns.

Nature and mental wellbeing

While this relationship remains largely ignored, there are proponents that focus on the potential of healing in nature and more broadly on the positive impacts that being in green space have on wellbeing. Berger and McLeod (2006) and Jordan and Marshall (2010) provide introductions to ways of incorporating nature into therapy and highlight the benefits of being in nature. The Sustainable Development Commission in the UK, which was closed by the coalition government in 2011, highlighted research that suggested that people with access to outdoor green spaces have fewer mental health problems and that being in nature has restorative effects (Sustainable Development Commission 2008).

Emmy van Deurzen describes how 'immersion in nature (walking, gardening, sailing, for example) has tremendously positive effects on all human functioning' (Deurzen 2008, p. 54). Higley and Milton (2008) found that 'even brief contact with the natural world provides relief from stress' and that 'there are also longer term, more profound benefits to be gained through contact with the natural world' (Higley and Milton 2008, p. 36). Hicks, a chartered counselling psychologist, concurs: 'I think it can have important implications for our sense of self experiencing a true connection with the world around us' (Hicks 2008, p. 7).

Literature, both old and new, shows that being in nature can potentially be transformative, but even our language makes articulating such experience difficult with its focus on distinction, definition and separation. Throughout this book I will endeavour to challenge this separation and ask that you aim to suspend the more normal view of nature as 'out there', as if we are not an integral part of the natural world. It is only through acknowledging and embracing our beings as cells in the body of nature that we can begin to be curious about how paying attention to this aspect of our being has the potential for a changed understanding of our experience of self. A focus on the nature of our existence is the starting point for beginning to move towards a shift in attitude to our illness, health and wellbeing.

3

The Importance of Place

And forget not that the earth delights to feel your bare feet and the winds long to play with your hair.

Kahlil Gibran (1926/1991, p. 47)

It is not usual for us, on any sort of regular or routine basis, to consider just how important place is to our sense of wellbeing. The changes to how and where we work and live that have happened over the last 100 years have impacted on our relationship with our natural world and how connected we are to, and how we feel about, our environment. What does it mean to feel 'at home' in a particular place? How does place relate to emotional experience and wellbeing and how might we address this with our clients? We will begin to examine how place might impact on our emotional and cognitive functioning and what happens when a person feels discon- nected from their wider environment. How might we address this in therapy? We will look at more practical steps that we might take to help us and our clients address the role of place in our existence. Not least, we will address where we practise therapy and the impact that this might have on the experiences of our client relationships.

Changing places

If I were writing this chapter 50 years ago or before, the chances are that it would have been something of a different experience. I would perhaps have been holding a pen and writing these words on a manuscript; I might have posted a draft to my publisher and waited weeks for written feedback. In the time between posting drafts and waiting for feedback I might have done a multitude of tasks, or none. The industrial and technological advances that have made our twenty-first century life barely recognizable to our ancestors have at the same time transformed our experiences on all fronts, shifting the nature of how we encounter the world, ourselves and each other.

Where we live, eat, sleep and breathe is as important as *how* we do and experience all of those things. In today's world, viewed through the lenses of the technology of the scientific age, we approach our lives and day-to-day activities as if the 'where' does not really matter very much at all. When we examine our lives, our experience of being in the world, we tend to approach it through what we can quantify. How much do we eat? How often do we sleep? For how long? How much do we weigh? The internet and self-help bookshelves are full of advice on what the 'norm' measurement for our lives might look like, and how we might aspire towards and attain the optimal amount. The *where* of our lives – the places where we eat, sleep, breathe, feel and relate to our ourselves and each other – is too often missing from the equation and evaluation. There is a common underlying assumption that transplanting life from one location to another, from one medium to another, will have little impact on the quality of our interactions, relationships and the sense of who and how we are. Place, the physical environment, is not brought into the discussion around mental and emotional health and wellbeing.

The technological advancements of the last century have provided huge benefits to us on a diverse range of fronts. They have removed much of the toil and hardship from physical labour, enabled us to connect across countries and continents, and facilitated massive strides in medicine, manufacture and our ability to garner facts and information. But at the same time, a direct impact of technological advancement is that we are distanced further from the earth, from our physical being. Technological advancements in manufacturing and farming mean that it is entirely possible to mentally deny the dirt and soil that is the origin of our food. The relationship that our ancestors might have had with the land, whether directly or indirectly, is diminished in our current age. Indeed, with modern farming practices, even for those directly involved in the farming of the fruit, vegetables, meat and fish that make it to our table, there is a much more sanitized relationship with the earth and land. That is not to critique these practices or advances (that might be for another time and place); rather it is to paint the backdrop to a picture in which the physical environment and the world are no longer deliberately considered with importance as they once were. They are no longer revered.

The status quo is that we are far less likely now than ever before to shine a light on our relationship with nature in any routine way. We are less likely to attend to it either for our individual or reciprocal wellbeing. The natural world is at best approached from the environmentalist vantage as a *thing* that we are destroying and that we need to begin to protect and at worst as a disposable resource that will forever keep providing for our insatiable needs. The physical environment is being viewed as a stage on which the play of our lives is performed, rather than an integral part of the unfolding of existence. Nature has become a thing that we are disconnected from and if we do pay her heed, for the majority of us it tends to be as either the subject of our climate concerns or as a brief excursion into an almost other-worldly place. Exercise 3.1 focuses on introducing us

Exercise 3.1 Becoming aware of place

This exercise can be completed in pairs or it can be approached as a self-reflective individual exercise.

Take a few moments to look around where you are sitting reading this. Be aware of what you are feeling, thinking and sensing. Spend a few minutes noting the quality of the place that you are in right now.

- What are the characteristics that stand out for you?
- What sights, sounds and smells attract your attention?
- How do you feel in this place?
- Are you aware of any particular memories or associations?
- Do you want to be in the place?
- How do you feel about being in this place at this time?

Spend some time jotting down the detail of your awareness and then explore (or reflect upon) what you have noted.

to the idea of place and offers an opportunity for reflection on how we consider place. This is particularly useful in client work to enable awareness at a wider level than might be usual and to facilitate movement outside of a firmly boundaried 'self' focus.

History and place

The nature of the changes described above that have altered the way we live also mean that we are less likely to have a longer-term, more enduring relationship with the specific places where we live and work. Again, wind back to half-way through the last century and I might be working in a town where I had been born and raised, perhaps also where my family and previous generations had lived and worked. The places in which we live and work now have far less of a generational meaning than they had in previous times. While this is widely known and written about, it is usually with the aim of reflecting on how we might be disconnected from *other people*, rather than with the place of our experiences. If we make the assumption that a connection with our past is integral to shaping who are, is a constituent of how we define ourselves, then we can also begin to consider how having a connection or not with a *place* through our history might also influence our sense of self. Exercise 3.2 encourages an exploration of place in childhood and gives an example of how we might conduct place exploration both in therapy and as a self-development exercise.

Exercise 3.2 Place and historical connection

This exercise considers historical connection with particular places. It can be expanded to become the focus of a psychotherapy session. Equally, it can be adapted to include in initial assessment sessions.

Focus for a moment on the idea of 'childhood home'. Is there one particular place that stands out for you? Perhaps there is more than one place, or perhaps there is nowhere specific.

▶

Try to settle on one particular image of place that is relevant to when you were a child.

For a few moments focus on the image or place with as fine a detail as you can.

Note down or draw the key qualities of the place, paying particular attention to sensory experiences, colours, tones, textures.

- What is your overall sense of being in that place?
- How do you feel taking yourself to that place and being aware of it now?
- What does this place mean to you?
- What would it be like to be reading this, completing this exercise, in the place that you think of in relation to 'childhood home'?

Now, in pairs if that is practical, spend some time exploring how you relate to that place now. Notice if you yearn for the place or if you do not. Ask yourselves and each other.

- Are you attracted to similar or different places?
- Is there a thread running through how you feel about particular places that relates back to this place?

Place and being well

While place is not really considered on a formal basis when we consider the state of our emotional and mental health and wellbeing, anecdotally we pretty widely accept that the places that we live and work in do have some sort of an impact on how we feel; on our overall mood and resilience. Sunday supplements fall out of newspapers tempting us to beautiful, tranquil beaches and breathtaking mountain ranges, enticing us to spend money on journeying to places to be inspired, revitalized and relax. The sorts of places that tempt us through travel adverts – the sorts of places that we desire to be in – are for many of us far removed from where we reside. The majority of the population, at least in the UK where I write, live in urban or suburban environments. A study published in *The Guardian* (2018) highlights that by 2030 it is estimated that more than 92% of the

UK population will live in cities and the worldwide increase in the percentage of people living in cities is expected to continue to soar. While living in cities is not assumed to be a bad thing, and indeed has been cited to have many benefits (not least in terms of reducing average carbon footprint and maintaining contact with nature), being in the sorts of environments that naturally inspire, motivate and sustain us, is often harder and feels out of reach. Financial well-being comes into play too, since access to green spaces, to holidays and travel is dependent on purse strings.

There are several studies that show that people with access to 'natural' places feel better. In their study, Kaplan and Kaplan found that people with views of nature feel better in themselves physically, and their research reported that participants felt reduced levels of stress (Kaplan and Kaplan 1989). Studies also suggest that patients in hospital fare better generally if they have contact with nature, either in physical reality or even through viewing images of natural landscapes (Winter and Koger 2010). Exercise 3.3 encourages us to think about how we experience being in different environments and to reflect on our relationship with the natural world (I realize that to make a distinction between the natural world and any other kind of world can itself be problematic, and is also somewhat subjective). (Dot should come after the bracket).

Exercise 3.3 Being in natural places

A Guided Meditation

Ideally complete this exercise in a group, in pairs or as a therapy exercise. To begin with, have one person (or a group facilitator) to guide the other through the meditation. If you are the facilitator or therapist, spend a moment to read through the outline below and try to adapt or extend the focus as appropriate. Please allow for all people to be the focus, or discuss as a group how you will proceed fairly. Also allow adequate time for debriefing and reflection, since focusing on place can often be a powerful emotional experience.

Close your eyes and sit comfortably in your chair or on the floor. Inhale and exhale slowly a few times and become aware of your breathing.

Think about the place in the world that you would most like to be in right now.

▶

◀

You can be with anyone in that place, or on your own, so try not to be drawn to a location because of a person.

Think of the place. If several places come into your awareness spend a moment thinking about which one seems to draw you most strongly. Settle on one place if you can and imagine yourself in that place.

- Which one do you yearn for?

- What sort of place are you in?

- Are you sitting down or walking or lying down in your place?

- Be aware of your body and how you feel as you are in that place. Is your skin hot or cold?

- What is your breathing like?

- How do you feel? Content? Excited? Tranquil?

- What is your view? Continue to try and stay present in your special place.

- What are you doing in your place?

- What potential do you feel?

- Try to be as aware as you can of all that you are experiencing in this place. If there are not words that adequately express what you are experiencing, be aware of the felt bodily sense as well as the spiritual connection.

- Gradually return to being present in the room that you are in.

- Begin to imagine leaving the place, saying goodbye for now.

- What are you feeling as you begin to leave and return to the present?

- What are you going to miss about this place? In your own time and when you feel comfortable, open your eyes.

Spend some time exploring that experience. Focus on areas such as what it is like leaving the place. What does it show you about what matters to you? Do you feel different in different places? Is there anything that is hard to describe or that does not make sense to you? If there is, do not be tempted to ignore it or to fit it into inadequate words. Sometimes we have spiritual connections to places and words do not seem to be able to capture them all. We will discuss this later in Chapter 7.

Much of what we might see as mental health symptoms or emotional disorder are seen by some eco-practitioners as potentially being caused by, or at least related to, the way we live and our disconnection from nature. Hopefully in the guided meditation of Exercise 3.3 we have increased our awareness of how places might be at least part of how we feel. Buzzell and Chalquist (2009) write about the impact of disconnecting from nature on our emotional wellbeing and suggest that re-connecting with nature can impact on how we feel and on our mental health. The way that we go about this re-connection can vary hugely but might include taking part in retreats in the wilderness or being aware of how we are forcing ourselves to fit into artificial time schedules and perhaps thinking about the potential of relating to time in a more embodied, experiential way. Although wilderness retreats might not be available to everyone and often seem to require some degree of time or financial commitment that might seem out of reach, later we will look at how ideas from wilderness practice might be brought into day-to-day living and more mainstream psychotherapeutic practice.

Gemma's particular place – letting go, returning, connection

Gemma grew up in remote countryside near the sea, and only truly began to realize how important being in nature was to her when she moved to the city at the beginning of her adult years. Gemma reminisced to me about how important being on the beach was for her as she grew up. She remembered how being on her own was important to her – being able to sit outside, being still, dreaming.

Gemma has now returned to 'home', being near the sea, and she now experiences the similar sorts of feelings about that nature as she had as a child. Gemma had a rather powerful experience down at the shore, which remains important to her many years later. At this time, she was starting to explore her identity and meaning and was particularly focusing on the spiritual dimension of her life. She was curious about paganism and had started to be interested in crystals and had read that she needed to wash her crystals in the light of a full moon. Gemma bought three quartz crystals and she went to cleanse them, as she had heard that she should, in order to become in tune with them. She went to the sea in the moonlight to bath them. Holding them in her hands she let the waves lap over them before placing them in a shallow bowl on a rock. The water gently lapped over them and suddenly a large wave came along. As it receded it took them away. Lit by the moonlight, Gemma searched in vain and after spending a long time looking she decided that there was nothing that she could do.

Gemma felt that she had to understand what this deeply upsetting experience meant to come to terms and accept it, and she felt there was a learning about things getting taken away from her. The following morning she returned to the beach to look for the crystals, as she did over the course of at least three tides. Several days later, she returned to the same spot and all three crystals were near where she had originally lost them. Gemma said that she felt that she had been drawn to find them, that she was meant to let them go, and that having let them go she could then find them again. Since this time, Gemma has experienced that when she lets things go they either come back to her or come back in a slightly different way.

Gemma talked to me about how her relationship with nature is fundamental to her wellbeing, that nature brings her back to who she is, puts her in touch with herself, 'but without all the stresshead on'. She relaxes and feels at home in nature and it sustains her: it is where she feels that she can breathe fully. Although throughout her life this has often involved time spent on the beach, or in large expansive vistas, gardening has become a very transformative experience for Gemma. Gemma struggles to find words that convey the feeling of being at home in nature – words just don't seem to hit the spot. A feeling of freedom permeates Gemma's description, contrasting with being in the city where she feels enclosed. Peace accompanies this freedom, particularly related to getting away from social rules. Inherent in this freedom is the liberation of not being constricted in either space or time, particularly in terms of rules and routines. Gemma feels that the more space that she is in the less anxious she feels. Gemma used her hands to describe the expansive experience of being in nature, particularly near the sea. She said that when she imagines herself being outside in nature she wants to stretch her hand out wide to the side, that the experience is expansive and that she feels freedom and able to breathe slowly and deeply. All of the stress that she might be feeling and her worries seem to dissipate.

Gemma feels that her relationship with nature helps her maintain her sanity; it seems to nurture her and feeling its expanse is reassuring, affirming and empowering. When Gemma reflects on her experience of transformation in nature it is a very holistic experience, one that impacts on and involves her whole being and all of her senses. She talked about the sound of the waves crashing in, the visual stimulus of the green grass, the texture of the rocks, feeling the wind in her face.

Gemma feels that she loses part of a sense of self. While she still knows and is aware of herself, she feels merged in with the earth, with the environment, with trees and the cloud. She feels that everything is interconnected. This resonates with her spiritual philosophy of interconnection – that we are all part of each other, part of everything.

Being in nature seems to nourish Gemma's soul, restoring her equilibrium and helping her to feel deeply connected. Being completely at one with nature, at one with everything in the world, feels very valuable: there is a sense of spirituality that is difficult to articulate. Gemma suggested that this feeling comes close to utter serenity, a sort of Buddhist Nirvana.

Connection and disconnection

Modern life of the 2010s is characterized by an ever-increasing sense of being connected and available. For people born around the start of this century, the idea of not being in routine, almost permanent contact through technology is anathema. My mobile phone alerts me to someone who is requesting a connection through business networking. My iPad informs me that I have another friend request. My iMac, while I am sitting writing, tells me who is liking my tweets. Connection is central to the technological age and to our sense of who and how we are. Yet in some ways we are less connected than ever in our more transitory lives. I might have 500 friends on Facebook, but I have only met half of them at any point in my life and have an emotional connection with only a handful. The first part of Exercise 3.4 focuses on a client example. There is then space allowed for reflection on your own (or your client's) interpersonal connections, with particular emphasis on how physical places might relate to interpersonal relationships.

Exercise 3.4 Connection map

This exercise can be completed in pairs or individually and you will need paper and a pencil. In the centre of the paper draw a circle to represent yourself. In a spider diagram, think of all of the connections that you have and draw circles to represent each of these connections. You can choose whether to have a circle to represent groups of people (e.g., work colleagues) or individuals. Consider all aspects of your daily life and focus on anything that gives you a sense of connection. See a client example in Figure 3.1.

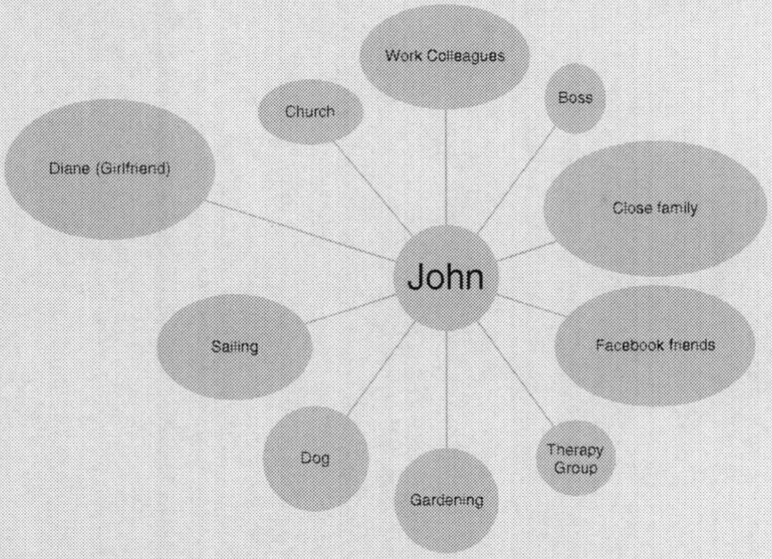

Figure 3.1   John's connection map

▶

◄

Are any of these connections related to particular places? What are the qualities of these places or this place? For example, John might describe the connection with the seasons that he feels when he is nurturing his garden. When he is away on business for extended periods of time he feels less grounded in nature because gardening is his connection to the natural world and to the sense of joy that he experiences living in a seasonal climate.

Now think about what each of these connections might mean to you (Figure 3.2). List the connections and draw your own map. Begin to think about what these connections mean to you and how they are important in your life, both on a daily basis and over the longer term. What would it be like to lose any of these connections?

Figure 3.2 My connection map

As we tend to focus on our health and wellbeing on an individual basis, it is widely acknowledged that the way we live can hamper our attempts towards greater wellbeing. Buzzell and Chalquist (2009) describe this well: 'the problem of our day is an inner deadening, an increasingly deployed defense against the stresses of living in an overbuilt industrialized civilization saturated by intrusive advertising and media, unregulated toxic chemicals, unhealthy food, parasitic business practices, time-stressed living, and (in the United States) a heart-warping culture of perpetual war and relentlessly political propaganda' (Buzzell and Chalquist 2009, p. 19). There are large parts of the status quo that Buzzell and Chalquist describe that are difficult to shift, and might require a gargantuan effort to consciously rally against. Yet if we begin to explore for ourselves and with each other what the connections that we have mean, and following on from that, those connections that we are lacking, we can move towards countering the inner deadening and alienation that results.

Being in nature provides a connection with the wider world, the value of which is often not given the seriousness that it deserves. If we consider for a moment what happens when a person is incarcerated in prison: what is the punishment that is prescribed? The freedom that is taken away is not just about the freedom of movement or the freedom to maintain interpersonal relationships. It is the freedom to breathe outside air, to have contact with the natural world, to experience the diversity of nature, to feel warmth or cold on skin, to see things through the clarity or haze of natural light. This deprivation can be as powerful as the deprivation of interpersonal contact. It is this deprivation that Linden and Grut describe as causing psychological damage, suggesting that 'if we do not consider ourselves connected with nature we are in a state of disconnection and this is what shattered lives are about. If we cannot make a link with what is outside ourselves, we cannot get to know ourselves. People who are imprisoned are starved of natural light, of fresh air, of contact with the natural world' (Linden and Grut 2002, p. 30).

Jung made practical suggestions in connection with our relationship with nature centred on ideas that would seem familiar to many of us today, such as working with the land, avoiding being swamped by technology, and the like. However, the purpose that he gave for these sorts of suggestions was not, as we might envisage, to help us to nourish nature and our environment; rather it was to 'let nature affect us' (Jung 1975, p. 19). Jung balanced the environmentalist stance to suggest that we let nature in to heal us (Jung 1975).

Where we practise therapy

When we think of therapy, we tend to think of two people sitting in a room across from each other. Invariably we practise indoors, sitting on chairs. So how might we begin to bring the idea that place matters to our emotional and mental wellbeing into our therapy practice, into the therapy hour (or 50 minutes)? To begin with we can consider our initial meeting with our clients and the physical environment that we bring them into. While it is not always possible or indeed desirable for us to change where we practise therapy, we can at least do a stock take of the environment in order to increase awareness of how it might impact on our client relationships and to consider if there are aspects that we feel we need to, or are able to, change. In Exercise 3.5 we will take some time to evaluate the physical space in which we endeavour to facilitate healing and exploration.

Exercise 3.5 A stock take of our therapy space

Whether we have been practising in the same space for some time or are relatively new to our environment, if we are to work from the premise that place matters, it is important to try and take a step back and examine what we are offering to our clients, and what messages we might be communicating through our therapy space.

1. Imagine that you are approaching your therapy room for the first time. Try and describe as accurately as possible what you are seeing as you arrive. What assumptions do you make about the practice? What messages do you receive from the physical environment?

2. You are sitting in your therapy room. Firstly, take stock of your own experience as a therapist. How do you feel in the space that you are sitting in? Focus hard on the details and what you might routinely ignore.

▶

◀

3. Look at the walls around you and focus on the textural quality of the room that you are in. Move around in the space. Contemplate the light and shadow, the textures, scent, the quality of the air, the surfaces. What do you usually take for granted? What have you become used to? How does your feeling about this space and place differ from how you might feel in other places? What would you change?

Once we have taken stock of our therapy space, we can begin to think about the impact of place on the therapy for the client. In order to do this it is helpful to reflect on an actual case example of being with a client (see Exercise 3.6). If this is not appropriate at this stage, reflect on an important recent interaction in a different setting.

Exercise 3.6　Place and a therapy session

Therapy practice

Consider a recent counselling or psychotherapy session that you have been in. The focus will be on the experience of your client. Were there any observations that you made about how your client felt in your room? Did your client make any observations about the space? Often when clients make observations about being in therapy we ignore the environmental or place aspect. Spend some time discussing anything that your client might have felt or remarked on that might be to do with being with you or in therapy. Does place come into this? What might happen if you shifted the room around? How do you provide space for your client in your room?

Now think about your client and imagine the sort of space that you feel would be healing for your client, or that would facilitate greater growth in your therapeutic relationship. Spend some time being as creative as you can as you consider this.

Place: A case illustration

Andrew is 50 years old and he lives in a market town in the South of England and sees a psychotherapist at a local mental health charity. At various times, Andrew has been diagnosed with a range of mental illnesses and takes medication for depression, anxiety, trauma and insomnia. Andrew came to therapy because, in spite of his rattling pill cabinet, he felt that his enduring struggles with living remained markedly unresolved. At his first meeting he described feeling tired, how lonely he felt, and how he really struggled to have any motivation to do anything. He had not felt able to work for several years. His psychotherapist initially followed the format of the assessment sheet provided by the charity where the therapy took place. This focused largely on Andrew's mental health and wellbeing, more broadly on his physical health (was he drinking, eating, sleeping and generally taking care of himself) and, importantly, whether or not he represented any risk to himself or to other people. There was no room on the assessment sheet for *the place* of where his struggle was happening. Andrew had previously served in the Armed Forces and had spent most of his time moving between many different locations.

At the start of his therapy Andrew was homeless, living rough in the town of his childhood. The assumption of his psychotherapist was that being homeless was negative, and yet further exploration and discussion with Andrew challenged this assumption. Through working with his therapist, Andrew began to explore place and what it meant to him. Andrew found it very difficult to be inside, and his anxiety increased and he felt less safe every time he felt forced to take part in and conform to an indoor life. Yet, his physical health was worsening whilst he was living in the streets. His therapy sessions focused on what it meant to him to live rough in that particular town. Although there were very obvious disadvantages to the place that he was living in, he also felt a historical connection with where he was living. He expressed a huge value to connecting to his life and to the memory of himself as he was before he joined the Armed Forces. Staying in the locality was important to him, though he recognized that he needed and wanted to be able to access support to move into accommodation at some point. Further exploration of how he felt in particular places related to the social dimension of place. He had been offered, and tried to accept, several places in shared rooms, yet these increased his hypervigilance and so he had repeatedly turned down this support. Other services had seen this as a rejection of help at some level, and indeed Andrew was convinced that it meant he might not be able to live or cope indoors at all. His psychotherapist helped him to explore the detail of the places and what they had felt like for him, and this in turn enabled him to have a more nuanced awareness of what he was experiencing. He realized that at that time he wanted to live in a supported environment but equally that he needed to be on his own in his own space, and to make his own environment feel safe and containing. With extra support services, Andrew moved into individual half-way house accommodation and was able to adapt to his environment, by moving furniture around, so that his room became reminiscent of the cocooned tent-like construction that had become his norm, and that for him, at that stage, represented safety.

Commentary

Place would probably have been the focus of discussion with Andrew, regardless of therapeutic orientation or of affording it more space in the dialogue. However, actively focusing on this dimension, rather than being exclusively focused on feelings, thoughts, depression or anxiety, allowed Andrew to give more time and thought to what mattered about different places and what they meant for him. Accepting that how he felt and what he thought about being in different places was an extremely important part of his therapy allowed him to lessen his sense of guilt and frustration for not accepting the hostel help that he was originally offered. Finally, his psychotherapist at least partially bracketed her own assumptions around what living in a particular place might be like or mean and around being homeless. This enabled the value of his homelessness to be expressed more openly by Andrew. It was only once this had happened that Andrew had a sense of what he needed and how he might think about his next move. This was an important step for Andrew, enabling him to feel in control of where and how he was living. Andrew developed a more holistic approach to his emotional and mental wellbeing, beginning to see it in the context of his environment and his circumstances, rather than just a product of his mind or of his own making.

Implications for practice

1. The 'where' of our psychotherapy practice matters. Although we cannot expect to routinely be able to change the actual environment

that we are in when we meet with our clients, we can acknowledge it as part of our therapy and the therapeutic boundaries.

2. The 'where' of the client's existence matters. Bringing in 'where' to therapy as much as 'how' or 'what' shifts the focus and widens awareness. Encourage reflection on the places in which people experience. Explore the difference between feelings and thoughts in different places. This will encourage clients to expand how they frame their experience.

3. Do not, whether intentionally or otherwise, rule out place as the central issue in any client material. It is all too easy to focus, for example, on depression as if it resides all in the mind, when in fact, some environments feel extremely depressing. If your client feels depressed by environmental issues, encourage exploration of potential small shifts that might make a difference.

4. When clients talk about feeling connected or disconnected, it is usual to assume that this relates to their relationships with other people. Make sure that you encourage discussion about connection to place.

5. Sometimes in psychotherapy we ask clients where they would like to be in a month, a year, five years' time. Yet often the implicit assumption behind this question relates to work, or relationship or feeling. Focusing more literally on *where* clients might like to be is as important as *what* they would like to be doing, and who they would like to be doing it with.

6. Encourage clients to think about the parts of the 'where' of their lives that they take for granted, and consider how these might come into focus or be up for exploration. What might it be like to walk a different route home, for example, or how might they make small changes to their daily environment that might facilitate a greater sense of wellbeing. Where might make them smile or feel calm?

7. Explore with clients the assumptions that they might hold about the place that they live in, if they feel that place is part of part of the construct of their depression or distress. What are they assuming might change if the place was changed? Does this feel realistic and how might it be achievable, at least at some level?

4

The Rhythms of Existence

Every moment of each of our lived existences is automatically situated in time. In the same way that we are always necessarily physically embodied in a place, so we are embodied in a particular place *in time*. At a very basic level, time is viewed as an abstract entity, some sort of numerical marker or a guide from which we arrange and locate our 'to do' list; a monitoring application to help increase our awareness to whether or not we should be attending to a physical, social, personal or indeed spiritual need. The alarm clock makes efforts to wake us up in the morning; the agenda alert on my mobile telephone reminds me that I am meeting a friend for lunch; the station clock invariably tells me just how behind schedule the Norwich to Liverpool Street Station train is running, my clinic clock warns me that my client session is about to come to an end and the beautiful church bells ring around the village, inviting me to the impending celebration and reflections of the Sunday service. We are all probably far too familiar with the importance of temporal awareness in relation to the management, categorization and dissection of our day-to-day lives. It is extremely useful to have functional time reminders notifying us of where we need to be, what we need to do; to be reminded of where we are situated temporally in each day, and indeed in the wider potential expanse of our lives. Yet this is only one particular aspect of the relationship that we have with time; time is much wider than its ability to demarcate, restrict and define.

Time is more than the metronomic, arbitrary ticking of hands, more than linear, forward progression and in this chapter we will consider the wider rhythm of time and think about how else time is important to us. How might we consider the nuanced rhythms of our existence and how might we consider the cadence of the natural world in relation to wellbeing and mental and emotional health? The writings of Minkowski (1933/1970) and Sartre (1946) together provide valuable insights into the relationship between depression, anxiety and temporality. The rhythms of the natural world impacts on us as practitioners and clients. What can re-connecting to these natural rhythms show us of our own bodily rhythm? How might we work with rhythm in psychotherapy and counselling?

Being in nature has the potential to help us return to the present and move towards a greater level of embodied, connected experience of our being in time. The present is always located in relation to our outer boundaries of time: the past point of our birth and the future inevitable moment of our physical death. This chapter will provide some practical ideas and activities in order to help us reflect on our place in time, ideas and activities that have the potential to assist feelings of being stuck and stagnation. Critically evaluating the choices that we have in relation to time helps us live more authentically, particularly in relation to facing the finitude of our existence. Scrutinizing the implications of the boundaries of time brings us face to face with our own mortality. Being in nature can facilitate a greater awareness and acceptance of these boundaries and our mortality. Although facing our own existential limitations and the idea of our own death might be difficult, it also enables us to live more vitally, once we accept and truly understand that we have only a finite amount of time on this earth, at least in our present forms.

The sensory awareness of being in nature allows us to be in touch with a rhythm that feels lost or absent in normal life and that facilitates being in touch with bodily rhythms, away from ideas, cognitions and ascribed meaning. Sometimes it takes time to get used to this rhythm, particularly when the schedules of social structures have routinely taken us outside of this rhythm.

Temporal being

Time is intrinsic to our fabric

The person that I am, the relationships that I have with myself, with other people and with the world around me are all situated in a particular place or particular places, as we saw in Chapter 2. Time is also central to our being. However much I try and describe myself or another person, what is happening in my environment, my work or play, I am to some extent caught out because *I exist in relation in time*. Without relating in time, I might be able to come to a position where I fully understand myself, get a grip of what matters to me, an enduring sense of who I am and where I am placed in the world. Yet time serves to throw any search for safety and certainty into the ether. For example, if I was trying to understand or describe an oak chair or a china vase, I might be able to arrive at a list of variables or a summary that could reasonably stand as an enduring definition over extended periods of time. The shade of the wood might deepen, the lustre of the vase shift, but the relationship that these objects have to their environment does not change so markedly in time as with us human beings. Time is so intrinsic to our being that we might consider that we are made *of* time as well as *in* it; it is one of the central ingredients of our make-up. There is no sense that can be made of our being without placing time at the centre. The constant change that we all live in, our evolution both personally and on a wider basis, has *time right at its core*.

Critiquing the change of culture and time

Change is a central tenet of mental health literature and the central project of the self-help book shelves and of many people's ideas about the purpose of therapy. Whether they are addressing changing physical habits, eating and drinking, or attempting to make changes to what they see as an aspect of their personality, change is a very common theme and desire. 'How can I become a better parent, a more loving husband, a better lover?' 'I want to be more confident at work/in my social life.' The change wish list can be endless and exhausting. As psychotherapists, we know that many of the people that cross the thresholds of our clinics are approaching us to help them to change something. To differing degrees they consider it their own responsibility to change. We will explore the notion of fixedness and fluidity later in this chapter, but to begin with I urge us to reflect for a minute on the assumptions that underpin the idea of change.

The assumptions of change

The assumptions behind ideas of change include the proposal that there exists a variety of relatively fixed ways of being in the world. The principle of change seems to me to be that we move *from* something *to* something else. There is a point of departure that is my starting point (perhaps I feel that I have an unhealthy diet, or that I am disorganised, a controlling wife or an disconnected mother) and I wish to move to a different place - the point of arrival (to feel healthy, immaculately organised, an equal spouse or a kinder mother). At the risk of labouring the point with a somewhat far-fetched example, I might seek therapy with the aim of wanting to change from being the wooden table to a delicate vase, holding the assumption that the change or transformation is possible, but noting that my intention and desire is still to move from one fixed way of being to another fixed way of being.

On New Year's Day each year many of us make resolutions (or perhaps intend to but never quite get around to it) to be different kinds of people or to behave in different kinds of ways. While the particular details of the resolution of any kind of change might provide a very useful insight into what each person needs, desires or dislikes, spending some time thinking about how an individual views the *process* is equally valid and potentially very insightful. Exercise 4.1 is helpful in providing insight into our experience, and can be a useful tool at the beginning of psychotherapy with new or potential clients in understanding their worldview, motivations and intentions.

Exercise 4.1 Understanding a person's assumptions of change

1. Outline briefly what and how you would like to be different.

2. How do you see yourself at the moment, before these changes?

3. How would this difference/these differences impact on your life and how you see yourself?

4. What do you see needing to happen for this change to take place?

5. How do you imagine this process happening?

6. What if this change is either not possible, or never happens?

Moving from the idea of being fixed

The moment that I try to define myself, to understand in anything other than a fleeting way this life I live and the relationships that I have, time sits on my shoulder, reminding me that we are all, always, in a constant process of evolving. Sartre summed up this sense of not being fixed, static beings beautifully in his book *Existentialism and Humanism*: (Sartre 1946). Sartre wondered 'What do we mean by saying that existence precedes essence? We mean that man first of all exists, encounters himself, surges up in the world – and defines himself afterwards' (Sartre 1946, p. 29). What Sartre is saying is that the self that I define myself as, and the self that you define yourself as, arise from our being in the world and in relationship *at a particular moment in time*, rather than existing as permanently defined entities existing outside of context and temporality. From this vantage point we can think of time as being an intrinsic part of our structure and make-up, rather than an abstract concept. When we considered the assumptions underlying how change is perceived or approached we noted that often we consider the movement from one fixed state or way of being to another fixed point. This is at least in part because of the absence of both time and context from the equation.

We all carry around images of who we think we are and who we think other people are that are based on enduring ideas of how we have previously seen ourselves and how other people have cast us in certain lights. I sit in my psychotherapy clinic and I hear on a regular basis how self-identity and self-image are stuck at particular moments, particular points in time. In Chapter 7 we will look at self-identity, but for now let us begin to think about how we sediment experience in time and how being in nature and paying heed to the natural world might confront the all too familiar sense of being stuck (see Exercise 4.2).

Exercise 4.2 Client session exploring self-identity and photographs

(This exercise can also be useful for exploring our own personal material.) Ask your client to bring in to a session, or to think about, a favourite photograph of themselves. Work on the following questions:

1. What is it that you like about yourself in that photograph?

2. What characteristics do you feel are being expressed or presented?

3. Do you feel and/or think that you are different in any way to the image that is presented in the photograph?

4. Do you feel and/or think that you are similar in any way to the image that is presented in the photograph?

5. To what extent do you try and hold on to this idea or image of yourself both for yourself or for other people?

6. Spend some time focusing on how you feel right now. To what extent is your present experience similar to or different from the photographic image?

7. Are there particular places that seem to foster the feelings that resonate with the photograph? Indeed, what is the felt experience of the place you are in in the photograph?

Time and depression

Modern psychiatric classification systems, such as the American Psychiatric Association's Diagnostic and Statistical Manual V (DSM V) (American Psychiatric Association (APA) 2013) or the World Health Organization's International Classification of Diseases (ICD-10) (World Health Organization 2016), have an array of measurement criteria for classifying and defining mental ill health. The categories that cover what we broadly understand as depression include a range of individual specifiers. Deurzen's phenomenological description of depression is considerably more holistic (Deurzen 2009). Deurzen describes the experience of depression as 'a feeling of deflation, a sense that there is a lack of something, outside or inside oneself, and usually in both at once' (Deurzen 2009, p. 99). A person that is in this state of mind and body has lost much of a sense of hope and has relinquished something of their aspirations and future focus: this sense of despondency 'will press one further down and lead to further deprivation' (Deurzen 2009, p. 99). Importantly, Deurzen captures the *lack* of something outside as well as inside: we are all familiar with descriptions of what it is like to be depressed that focus on the perceived inner workings of the mind. Deurzen shows us the connection, or lack of connection, with the outer world, the broader environs, that is also part of what it means to be in a depressed state.

The experience of depression is one of a loss of energy and lack of motivation, with a perception of barrenness. To greater or lesser extents, some qualities of these experiences are part of what it is to live. Sometimes we feel as if we are full of energy, hopeful, loved and optimistic and at other times we are likely to feel unmotivated, lethargic, despondent and overall rather hopeless and subdued. Deurzen describes how our emotional experiences come in cycles and are part of our fluid connection *to the world* (Deurzen 2009). It is when our emotional experiences become fixed, stagnant and enduring that they become problematic. It is when the smaller constituents seem to fuse together into an enduring state that we start to describe the experiences as depression. There is a problem with trying to fix ourselves, extracted from the fluid rhythms of time as personalities or selves, that has an inherent potential danger of moving us into a stuck way of being.

If we think of ourselves as part of a connected system, porously boundaried entities rather than heavily defined beings, then we begin to free up who we are and how we describe our living. To some extent we need to define ourselves as beings, in order to know ourselves and not to be 'nothings'. If we return to Sartre's idea that existence precedes essence: although his words imply that any essence we capture of ourselves is relational and only defined after the fact, he still shows us that part of what it is to be human and make sense of existence is to create essence (Sartre 1946). Sartre accounts for the experience of inner and outer lack that is clearly part of depression through how he conceives 'the self': 'If man as the existentialist sees him is not definable, it is because to begin with he is nothing' (Sartre 1946, p. 28). Not only does Sartre explain these feelings of lack, he suggests that conceiving ourselves as something, as a defined entity, is itself deception: while 'we love to act as if we are set and substantial' this is itself an example of the kind of self-illusion that Sartre defines as 'bad faith' (Sartre 1943, pp. 45–47). From a Sartrean perspective the feeling of inner lack that is part of depression is an expression of a fundamental awareness of existence, *a priori* to definition or construction of self.

Sartre's ideas challenge the 'depression = illness' correlation: perhaps the 'sickness' might reside in the individual and collective pretence of objectifying a 'something' from which we then cast experiences of nothingness and lack as maladaptive. If we view ourselves as impermeable fixed beings, without taking account of our inter-relatedness to nature and the world, we miss potential sources of both distress and healing. In essence, we limit our experience. It is only by first acknowledging that we are part of the seasons, part of the passing of night and day, subject to and part of the same natural fluidity that we acknowledge as being important to the rest of nature, that we can begin to appreciate ourselves as rhythmic beings. Exercise 4.3 provides a starting point for reflecting on the potential of viewing ourselves with a similar fluidity as we do the rest of the natural system.

Exercise 4.3 Passing clouds, sunlight and heavy skies

This exercise is best completed outside, although if this is not possible find a space and a view that connects you to outside, and particularly to the sky. Use a voice recorder or a notebook to document your thoughts.

1. To begin with, take a glance, a snapshot, at the sky outside. Now close your eyes and capture in your mind the sky above you (or outside if you are inside). Once you have a clear picture in your mind of the sky make some notes and comments that describe the image.

2. Once you have documented that first description, open your eyes and focus on the sky again, this time for several minutes. As you sit or lie quietly and observe, describe what you see in the sky in as much detail as possible and make notes of your observations. If your mind wanders, try to focus back on as pure a description as possible.

3. Read or listen to what you noted in both 1) and 2). How were these experiences different from each other? What do they show you? What happens if you take a fixed, single view of the sky, yourself, or your relationships compared to if you try and describe and observe on an ongoing basis what is unfolding?

4. Consider how it might be possible to hold a fluid sense of who you are (what the sky is like at this moment) while staying open to shifts, light and dark.

Anxiety and time

Anxiety is experienced as an extremely physical state of being: the sweaty palms, tense stomach and raised heart-rate are part of what we understand as being anxious. From a medical perspective, anxiety is perceived as a disorder and extensive efforts are made to overcome or banish symptoms (American Psychiatric Association (APA) 2013). Breathing exercises, mindfulness, meditation and stress management are all employed in the fight against the anxious experience. From an existential-phenomenological perspective, anxiety is not quite so quickly banished, which is not to say that the intense discomfort of the experience goes unrecognized – far from it. Rather it is that anxiety is positioned as an integral part of the heart of existence: a fact of what it is to be alive in time (Cohn 1997; Deurzen and Arnold-Baker 2005). If we take Kierkegaard's view of the phenomenon, the more that we embrace anxiety the more likely we are to realize our possibilities (Kierkegaard 1844/2014). According to Kierkegaard, anxiety is our awareness of freedom – awareness of all of our possibilities and the infinite choices that we face through our being in the world (Kierkegaard 1844/2014). Existential philosophers and practitioners propose that maintaining something of our anxiety, rather than trying to banish it, is of potential value to us in living conscious and deliberate lives. Heidegger's particular take on anxiety suggests that the anxious experience confronts us with both the pseudo-securities that we maintain in order to make us feel comfortable (for life to seem acceptable and bearable) and with the real potential of our non-being: the point of our death (Heidegger 1962).

Being in wild nature, in the outdoors, is widely documented as helping alleviate anxiety and enhance mood and provide relief from everyday stressors without making us feel that we are smothering the truth about the limitations of lives (Mind 2007; Buzzell and Chalquist 2009). A good deal of the exercises in this book tend towards some sort of alleviation of anxiety through slowing down breathing, being more present, being outside and particular kinds of focusing (see Exercise 4.4). However, acknowledging our existence as part of the natural world also has the potential to help us to face the existential truths that Heidegger and Kierkegaard highlight, rather than automatically trying to banish this anxious experience, and to place them within a wider spatial, temporal and spiritual context.

A personal vignette

When I was at the start of my heuristic research into transformative experiences in nature during my doctoral training, I spent some months grappling with what it was I was feeling about the phenomenon; considering the detail of the question that was emerging. On a regular basis over several months I used to drive for a couple of hours westwards along the M4, across the Severn Bridge into South Wales, and head up to Storeys Arms Car Park at the foot of Pen Y Fan in the wet and wild Brecon Beacons. These trips seemed to coincide with a grey, overcast and rather depressing autumn landscape and yet I felt drawn to those hills in all of their cloud-drenched bleakness. My home at that time was in Hampshire, so I could equally have immersed myself in the South Downs, the New Forest or the Jurassic Coast, but something about the bleakness of Pen Y Fan seemed to keep calling me to immerse myself in it.

On one particular Friday, armed with my trusty voice recorder, I ascended the cobbled path over the first lower summit, watching the dots of the cars below recede into the distance as I left behind the faint hum of the road. As I rounded the first corner, saying good-bye to the sights and sounds of civilization below, I found myself walking from grey though relatively clear skies into the midst of thick, swirling, enveloping fog. I found myself quite overwhelmed and simultaneously rather scared and awestruck as vision seemed to disintegrate. One of the most vital moments that stood out for me was an awareness of the clouds constantly moving around me, being blown through me, and knowing that I was part of this ever-changing, moving world. In this succession of somewhat ethereal moments I became deeply aware of the passing of time, of my temporal connection to the world and to my ancestors, and of the transitory nature of my existence. At the same time I felt deeply anxious. I resisted the strong temptation, and my natural inclination, to turn around and retreat into the peace of clearer skies. Instead, I stood in the face of the choices that I was making, the knowledge of my place in history and the small amount of time I have on this planet compared to the time that the earth under my feet has had. This was not a completely pleasant transformative experience, of the kind I had perhaps been looking for or had had on previous immersion experiences, and it was a struggle to stay connected, present and immersed. Yet, this anxious experience urged me to face some very difficult personal questions about my motivation for choices I was making on a personal level and how much I was avoiding some uncomfortable truths. Had I focused on trying to withdraw from my experience of anxiety, through the sorts of control or avoidance exercises with which we are all too familiar, I would not have confronted myself or allowed myself the opportunity to experience the catalyst that I felt.

Shortly after the times where I had been routinely driving down the M4 and striding up Pen Y Fan for my research, my first husband was, completely out of the blue, diagnosed with incurable, inoperable brain cancer, and I found myself facing experiences and fundamental questions about what matters in life, in dying and in death. I found myself confronted with questions, feelings and a depth of pain that I would never have imagined being able to cope with and endure and contain, particularly in relation to the shock and grief of my children. My experiences of standing on that mountain, merging with the clouds, connected to time and to relatives long-since passed, facing some sort of truth of existence, helped me greatly as I grappled with making sense of my life and my being thrown into a situation in which I felt extremely helpless, out of control and deeply anxious. At times during his illness, around his death and afterwards I felt more anxious than I had thought humanly possible, truly connected into the raw fragility of life. After his death I returned for occasional forays into those mountains, both on my own and with close friends, and I realized that I was much more able to be with my feelings openly and honestly in wild nature than in any other place. I found that facing truth, rather than trying to run away from it, is ultimately a liberating experience, even if that liberation is simultaneously a leap into pain and a confrontation with distress.

As I reflect on my personal experiences it seems important to me that we do not assume, as psychotherapists or for our clients, that any foray into the hills or wilderness experience will be a peaceful one or that it will feel positive and uplifting. Transformation and therapeutic experiences can be painful. Honestly confronting existence is very often deeply challenging. The nature that we are part of is beautiful and frightening. It is complex and requires us to proceed with cautious, informed and open-minded footsteps (Beringer 2004).

Finitude: birth, death and life in-between

The marking of time and the hands of the clock are both a marker of our relationship to, or distance from, our birth and at the same time a marker and symbol of our projection towards our death. John Donne's famous death bell, in Meditation 17, does indeed toll for all of us (Donne 1623). Existential philosophers and psychotherapists, such as Emmy van Deurzen, encourage us to live actively in the knowledge that our existence will cease at our death (Deurzen 2012). Through the seasons, through experiencing sunrises and sunsets, we become more in tune with the existential boundaries of our time, 'of birth and death and the life-giving warmth of the sun' (Brazier 2011, p. 47).

I have found that my personal relationship with nature has provided me with an emotional and existential metaphor of turbulent storms being weathered inside and out. As well as being at times healing and positively transformative, at times my trips into the mountains have, as I described earlier in this chapter, awakened other vulnerabilities – particularly affirming death and the transitory quality of each moment.

Watching the wind push the mist over the peak of a mountain, or listening to the rhythm of the tide retreat and advance, reminds and re-connects us with the finite boundaries of our existence as we know and understand it. 'Encountering life and death, growth and change, we experience things which are sometimes disturbing and other times uplifting, but always grounding' (Brazier 2011, p. 31). As the leaves fall off trees, or the buds break through after the last frost, we are reminded that we are alive in a present that is ever-changing: we are grounded in a finite experience.

In modern life we are shielded from much of the reality of human existence, maintaining an illusion that we are safe from our fears – particularly the most primitive fears of destruction and death. Being in nature reminds us of these fears and their basis in the reality of our existential boundaries, helping us to accept and harness our anxieties, urging us to live the life that we have now.

Natural rhythms

Our days are divided up into chunks of time related to bodily functions, work and education commitments and social activities. We have bathtimes, bedtimes, mealtimes, social times, clocking on and off times. Some of these are more loosely related to nature's rhythms than others. Sometimes we feel in tune with these rhythms, for example when a mealtime falls when our stomachs tell us that we are hungry, and sometimes we feel more disconnected from these rhythms and time expectations. Being a parent to pre-teens and teenagers is a very stark reminder of how imposed time boundaries can change mood and feel like a very uphill battle. During the term-time weeks the alarm clock goes off at around 7 am and the battle to do all that is required before departure for the school bus seems to be a fight against an overwhelming physical need to stay in bed. At the weekends, when there are no other commitments that demand early rising, the same teenagers will very happily sleep through until the sun is well over the yard arm. When they do eventually surface, waking with their body clocks, they are much happier versions of their Monday morning, 7 am selves.

The rhythmic importance of being in nature touches people in different ways at different times, from the immediate, as the wind blows clouds and cobwebs away and opens up a new vista, to the longer-term passing of time as seasons mark the ends and beginnings of years. When we awaken in the wild to the wonder of nature it can sometimes feel like a revelatory experience. Many people move from indoor experience to indoor experience, from home to car to tube, or home to bus to school, with limited immersion in and awareness of nature's rhythms (Brazier 2011). Yet if we make even small efforts to increase our awareness we can begin to consider how it might impact on us.

Return to the present through getting out into the natural world

Many people have documented their accounts of nature experiences that suggest that being in nature, particularly for extended periods, results in some sort of a shift in the experience of time: one of the most commonly described experiences is a sense of timelessness (Harper 1995, p. 192). The experience of time in nature is described as becoming 'less linear and more cyclic', opening up what is experienced as a 'new and different world' (Harper 1995, p. 183). Many of our more routine approaches to time are based on the ticking of a clock, checking off appointments and aiming ourselves towards impending deadlines, so that time becomes a measuring tool. It is as if time is artificially imposed onto the daily lives that we lead. But nature has her own time, her own expression of time, and Carl Jung wrote about the experience of being out of kilter with nature and nature's time (Jung 1969). Jung said that 'It is as if our consciousness had somehow slipped from its natural foundations and no longer knew how to get along on nature's timings' (Jung 1969, p. 802). Of course, we are part of nature, so Jung is suggesting that we no longer really know how to get along with our own natural time, our own foundations. In accounts of immersion experiences in nature, two important temporal themes emerge: being present and historical context (Roszak, Gomes and Kanner 1995; Brazier 2011). Being present and attending to the detail in the natural world slows us down from what can sometimes feel like a frenetic pace, helping us to reawaken our too often silenced natural bodily rhythms. We are alive in a particular moment, and focusing on the experience of being when we are in nature, removed from the normal rush of life, helps us put to one side anxieties about the future or regrets of the past, lightens our spirits and remind us of a present that matters.

Being in the moment for Edur

Edur lives in a region famous for its peaks and its extensive dramatic mountain ranges. One of his favourite places is a ski area very close to where he lives which is noted for some of the finest skiing in the world. Edur skis regularly with a group of friends; being outdoors is an essential and integral part of Edur's life. Edur skis in an environment that offers the opportunity to be in total wilderness. In day-to-day life, Edur finds it hard to calm his mind and experience really being in the moment. He described how, when he is in the mountains, everything seems to slow down and he is much more perceptive and aware of the present.

One day Edur described how he made a substantial effort to be in wild remoteness, venturing far from the beaten track to a place that he had heard described as pretty awesome – famous for utopian, champagne powder snow. Preceding this particular experience, Edur had had an emotionally turbulent time. He had experienced family bereavements, had recently finished a very difficult graduate school programme and he felt that he was just emerging from a period of trauma and chaos. On this occasion Edur and his friends decided to go to a particular ski area that was unfamiliar to them and which was remote from the main area. Edur described getting to the top of this bowl and how he felt that it was a very beautiful, surreal scene before him. He described a hazy sunshine with the sun shrouded by little wisps of clouds, almost like a light fog sitting over the bowl itself. Trees were shrouded in snow with sunlight peeking through the branches. The snow was glistening and the vista seemed wonderfully magical, almost unreal.

There was nobody else around, and the four friends looked at each other as Edur described asking himself 'could this be heaven?' as he marvelled at how magical the moment was. Time seemed to stand suspended in this moment, the scene felt ethereal, magically pivoted on the edge of reality. It was like floating on a cloud and felt particularly transformative after the personal chaos of the previous couple of years. Edur realized that this was the first time for a long time that he could hear himself think in the moment and feel present in his surroundings. The noise and chaos of previous years seemed to dissipate. Nature seemed to help him let go, as if being present was the only option in such awe-inspiring beauty. Just being present was very powerful, and in such contrast to his previous experience over the preceding years. This was very different from his usual experience of skiing. He seemed to float down the mountain, whereas usually he felt every part of the ground directly underneath him. This floating felt effortless, as if gravity, momentum and snow were carrying him along. This moment felt surreal, and he said that he felt he just had to let the moment carry him down the mountain. Edur felt a deep connection to a great whole, a connection that he experienced as deeply spiritual.

As well as Edur's experience in the beautiful snowy mountains Edur also discussed having an experience that shared some essential qualities when he was in the Greek Islands. He was swimming in the blue waters of the Mediterranean and felt that he had to pinch himself because it felt unreal, dreamy and magical.

From experiences such as these and living in an environment that puts a very high priority on being outdoors, Edur begun to realize how much he needs that time outside in nature as an ongoing part of his future life in order to bring some moments of peace, and to give balance, a sense of being in rhythm and a very different, powerful self-awareness.

Edur feels that usually he is quite control-orientated in his life. When he is nature, Edur feels immersed in the present and lets go of ideas of self-control. At these times he does not feel self-conscious and ceases observing himself, how he looks or sounds, for example. He is aware of who he is, that he knows himself, and that he does not have to do anything with himself. Being in nature has shown Edur something about balance in life and he also feels that these experiences in nature have shown him that there is also a rhythm to who he is as a person. Being still and taking in the moment is powerful and important. In that stillness there is a knowledge that everything will still be waiting; that stopping and turning off is very therapeutic.

Part of the transformational nature of this experience related to experiencing a shift in time. Through the feeling of being very present, after several years of painful times and chaos, Edur realized that nothing lasts forever – either the painful times or the very precious moments. This provided relief from the prospect and experience of difficulties and a feeling of needing to enjoy and savour the magic of the present moment. There are two sides to the impermanence of life that Edur is shown in nature. Nothing lasts forever: this is both a relief and an urgency to live.

Edur's experience in the mountains has impacted on how he views life, the choices that he makes and the direction that he takes, particularly in terms of feeling an active participant in his journey. Edur suggested that being reintroduced or reminded of the world beyond his own contextual experience relates to the sense of urgency that he feels and his increased awareness of the choices that he makes in terms of how to live.

Being in nature shifts us to a more present focus and helps us to slow down our thoughts and experiences, particularly those related to outside of the moment. It is widely documented in the writings of the eco-psychologists that the whirring of the brain seems to slow down and that thoughts seem to move at a much slower rate: gradually there is a distinctly peaceful meditative quality to experience (Metzner 1999; Winter and Koger 2010). Sometimes in the particularly turbulent periods of life that we will all encounter, being in nature provides a point of reflection where time seems to stand still for a moment, helping us to contain our worries and distress. Taking ourselves outdoors when we are in difficult periods of life shifts our perspective, seems to lift us, helps us make sense of things and work through what is happening in a more holistic, less analytical way. A friend of mine competes at quite a high level in the world of running. He describes how he goes trail running knowing that he has a question on his mind at the start of his two-hour run. At the end of his run, often he is much nearer making sense of whatever dilemma he is facing. And if he has not made sense of it, it seems to have a slightly less overwhelming flavour to it. Particular pathways and qualities of the forest trails that he uses to run seem to guide him in his thoughts in a way that does not seem to happen if he runs on the roads.

Exercise 4.4 Practical walking meditations

There are obviously many different ways to approach walking meditation. The most obvious basic suggestion is to put on some decent shoes and start moving outside. While there are still benefits from doing walking visualization meditations from the comfort of an armchair, these do not have the same benefits of connection that come from being outside in changing conditions, weather, sights, sounds and smells. If you decide to take clients outside as part of therapy, there are various websites and groups that offer practical guidelines around safety and boundaries. One might assume that walking meditation involves undertaking a decent amount of footsteps or must necessarily be outside, but there are various creative ways in which walks of a few steps can also be used.

1. Small Space Circular Reflection and Meditation

In a small outdoor space ask your client to begin in the centre of a circle (the client chooses the imaginary circumference). Ask your client to begin to walk in

▶

a spiral out from the centre of the circle while focusing on a particular troubling thought or feeling. Imagine leaving the thought, feeling or issue in the centre for a minute and ask them to begin to take steps away from it.

Ask the client to describe what is happening as they physically walk away.

Are there conflicting thoughts and feelings?

What images arise?

At what speed do they want to run or walk?

2. Cross-roads reflection

When clients have particularly difficult choices to make, ask them to stand at the junction of an imaginary cross-roads. One road is the result of one decision, the other the result of an alternative choice. Ask your client to deliberately walk down one of the routes at a time and discuss what happens for them, assuming that they have taken that decision.

What can they see?

Who is walking alongside them?

Who have they left behind?

What have they lost and gained?

What do the different horizons look and feel like?

Focus also on the physicality of the roads that they are walking along.

What does the horizon look like?

What colours are around them?

Do they feel drawn to the place or are they resisting moving forward?

Implications for practice

1. Time is much more than the ticking of the clock. It is part of our make-up and our relational living as part of the natural world. In our therapy practice we need to make sure that we pay attention to our clients' relationships to time. Time is so much more than the arbitrary 50-minute framework of a session or a schedule to stick to.

2. Being in nature can facilitate feeling more connected and present. Taking regular breaks in nature will help us recharge ourselves and can be an important part of self-care. Reflecting on whether or not our clients spend time outdoors can be as important as how they sleep and eat. Being in nature is sustaining and helps shift perspective.

3. So often the focus of people coming to counselling and psychotherapy is on trying to make changes in their lives, often to themselves. We need to encourage clients to think carefully about how they sediment themselves, both as they are now and as ideas of who they want to be. Reflecting on the constant shift of nature can provide a powerful mirror towards self-acceptance and an appreciation of the fluidity of life.

4. Being in nature can be transformative, yet at times this can be deeply painful as well as uplifting. This is a powerful metaphor for much of time. Encourage clients to view the whole of their experience rather than hiding the darker, stormy sides of life. It is the powerful wind that blows the clouds away.

5. The enduring landscape of wild nature can help clients (and us) connect to and accept grief after they (we) have been bereaved or when experiencing great loss. Sometimes the most powerful therapeutic experiences are wordless and unspoken; appreciating that birth, death, regeneration and disintegration are part of the cycle of the natural world can help facilitate some acceptance of experiences that sometimes seem too difficult to make sense of or comprehend.

6. Be as creative as you can in your use of ideas of natural movement, journeying and being in nature in your therapeutic work. While the therapeutic impact of wilderness therapy, adventure therapy and immersion experiences is well documented, weaving nature and a holistic approach to existence into more usual therapy environments can be equally valuable.

7. Do not assume that an experience in nature that is powerful for you will be meaningful for your client. The same nature that excites and liberates me might terrify my client, or at the very least leave them cold (and wet).

5

The Natural Body

We live in an age where our bodies are routinely objectified and manipulated. Whether in the guise of health or aesthetics, to varying degrees we approach our bodies as if they are constructed of clay; ready to be sculpted, shaved, coloured, injected with fillers and botox, tautened and dissected with the cosmetic surgeon's scalpel. We are often far removed from a feeling of being at home in our bodies; instead we are often ill at ease with our own physicality rather than comfortably inhabiting our own skins. At the same time as feeling a sense of disconnection from our bodies we are equally disconnected from the planet on which we live, the food that the planet provides us, the nourishment that provides the seamless continuity between us and how we grow and are sustained. In this chapter we will begin by looking at how we objectify both our planet and our bodies and we will explore the implications of this disembodiment. We will consider research that suggests that being in nature helps people feel that they are more *in* their bodies, as opposed to being external, judgemental observers. This chapter will draw on the writing of Merleau-Ponty (1962) in order to consider the nature of embodiment and the potential implications of these writings for wellbeing and health. Exercises will be proposed that help us move towards greater mind–body connection.

The writings of Laing (1960) will be considered in relation to potential psychological consequences of experiencing body and mind disconnection. Current mainstream psychiatric approaches to eating disorders will be evaluated and we will reframe what it means to nourish ourselves. Key questions considered will include:

> what can nature teach us about bodily awareness and acceptance?

> how can we help our clients feel that they inhabit a natural mind and body?

> what happens when clients feel disconnected from embodied experience?

> how can nature guide us in helping clients experience increased connection?

> how might embodied disconnection present itself in the therapy room?

The objectified planet – the roots of our disconnection

As we discussed in Chapter 1, we live in a world where, at least for the majority of us inhabiting the Western world, we go about our daily lives split from the nature that we are part of; split from our own nature. The experience of being disconnected from our bodies, of objectifying our physicality and to some extent our mental being, begins with the split from our roots. In his seminal work *The Voice of the Earth*, Theodore Roszak addresses the 'ecological unconscious' that is the repression that 'weighs upon our inherited sense of loyalty to the planet that mothered the human mind into existence' (Roszak 2001, p. 14). Roszak, along with many other eco-writers, is of the firm belief that much of our mental distress lies in our disconnection from our planet and our collective lack of ability or effort to see the needs of our planet and us as people as a continuum; connected and affected in myriad intricacies. Roszak proposes that if we consider psychosis as the attempt to live a lie then the 'epidemic psychosis of our time is the lie of believing we have no ethical obligations to our planetary home' (Roszak 2001). Yet even before we reach any conclusion about whether or not we have any ethical responsibility to our planet

and its other species and eco-systems, and whether or not addressing our planet's needs might help us reflect on and begin to heal our
own pains, we need to first acknowledge and understand the extent
of our current disconnection. We need to comprehend just how disconnected we are from the environment in which we are embedded
and how much we objectify our world as an inanimate being. It is
this understanding that is a prelude to the task of appreciating the
difficulties and continued pain and distress that comes for many us of
from approaching our bodies and physical being with such contempt.

Roszak (2001) reminds us that it is only our modern Western society that has split the inner life from the outer world 'as if what is
in us was not also inside the universe' (Roszak 2001, p. 14). Jordan
(2009b) suggests that we have developed a separation between nature
and ourselves to provide a safeguard, distancing us from our vulnerabilities and the reality of our actual dependency on earth. Laing,
writing in 1960, described the language that 'refers to man in isolation from the other and the world' or alternatively refers to 'falsely
substantialized aspects of this isolated entity' (Laing 1960, p. 19).

It is tempting to see the writings of the eco-therapists, eco-
psychologists and indeed Laing as novel or alternative. However, the
relationship between man and environment, looking to the earth
and environment for healing, guidance and sustenance, is embedded in ancient and modern indigenous and tribal cultures and rituals
and literature (Greenwood and Leeuw 2007; Higley and Milton 2008;
Roszak et al. 1995). I am inspired by Emerson's beautiful words, 'In the
wilderness, I find something more dear and connate than in streets or
villages. in the tranquil landscape, and especially in the distant line of
the horizon, man beholds somewhat as beautiful as his own nature'
(Emerson 1849).

Living on the planet, not as part of it

While I can make no specific assumptions about readers' environmental credentials or sensitivities, the fact that we are plundering our
planet for our own needs is a painful truth. Species across the planet
are endangered and dying out at a rate between 1,000 and 10,000

times higher than the natural rate of extinction, according to the World Wide Fund (WWF) for Nature (World Wide Fund for Nature 2017). It is tragic that scientists refer to our present age as the Sixth Extinction Wave in geographical history. The over-exploitation of our planet and its resources is completely unsustainable and yet we continue, largely unabated, to approach our relationship with our planet as if there are no long-term consequences for us or the earth, as if the earth is a production factory, automated to perpetually produce her goods to meet our over-consuming needs. Broadly speaking we behave towards the planet and its non-human inhabitants as if our demands are of no consequence, as if we can manipulate, burn, tear apart and attempt to rebuild, over-populate and heat it up without it mattering. We behave as if we expect no consequential damage as a result of our plundering earth's resources at any point in the system. If indeed we do admit that we expect the damage and destruction to have some consequence we largely behave as if we do not care very much.

Although we have seen that an existential approach does allow for our being embodied in the natural world in its philosophy, the relationship with our physical context is largely ignored when we consider mental health and emotional wellbeing. Higley and Milton point to how our being in nature is 'a neglected relationship in counselling psychology' and how this might relate to some of our present-day concerns and problems (Higley and Milton 2008, p. 10). Implicit in this statement is this reverse of the argument: that focusing on the relationship might be part of a resolution of some of these concerns.

To some extent, my writing perpetuates a sense of separation and is guilty of the species hierarchy that it attempts to challenge, since my intention is not to approach the nature of existence from all parts of the system, but primarily to focus on the human aspect part of the whole. Even if we do take a species-centric stance, in this case a human species stance, we can still allow for an appreciation of the whole and pay much greater heed to the context of our existence than might be assumed from reading much of the mainstream psychotherapy and mental health literature. If we take some time to consider that the earth and nature are the foundation from which we are born, we can begin to understand that approaching ourselves from a stance of fragmentation and separation might just have implications for our wellbeing on many levels: personal, social, cultural, emotional and spiritual. If we approach our planet with little regard, as an object worthy only of manipulation and exploitation, we are, at least implicitly, giving ourselves and each other something of a similar message. The effect of objectifying nature and the planet is that the seeds are sown for disconnecting and separating out the mental from the physical and for objectifying our bodies. This separation is in marked contrast to Merleau-Ponty's writing, which focuses on our being embodied *in the world* (Merleau-Ponty 1962). This resonates with the experiences that the eco-psychologists write about: that people spending extended time in nature feel more in touch with being embodied as well as feeling connected to, and part of, the wider system (Buzzell and Chalquist 2009; Brazier 2011; Macgregor 2013).

Mental disconnection and current approaches to psychiatry

In contrast to Merleau-Ponty's (1962) view of existence, the separation of mind and body, physical and mental health, is so deeply engrained in our society that it is hard to know where to begin in confronting the disconnection. It has not been forever thus: ancient approaches to psychologies were all what we might now narrowly categorize as eco-psychologies, holistically approaching mind, body, soul and world as one. The approach to mental health as separate from physical health is much more than a linguistic or categorizing split: a read-through of the fifth edition of the Diagnostic and Statistical Manual of Mental Disorders (DSM V) (American Psychiatric Association (APA) 2013), the psychiatrists' bible, shows an approach to mental illness and distress that assumes that the mind can be abstracted completely from body or world. There is not a single 'dis-ease' listed in DSM V, or indeed earlier versions of the same document, that connects mental wellbeing or ill health to the world in which we live (American Psychiatric Association (APA) 2013). The mind and the mental are objectified, separated off from the body and any environmental context. If this is how mind and mental health are classified it is of little wonder that limited lip-service is paid to nature and the wider environment in mainstream approaches to healing.

In his ground-breaking work *The Divided Self,* Laing discusses disconnection and fragmentation and how we 'take a single man in isolation and conceptualise his various aspects into "the ego", "the superego", and "the id"' (Laing 1960, p. 19). Laing describes how 'we have an already shattered Humpty Dumpty who cannot be put together again' (Laing 1960, p. 20). Laing makes a distinction between the embodied self and disembodied self, with the former having more of a starting-point for a 'different hierarchy of possibilities from those open to the person who experiences himself in terms of a self-body dualism' (Laing 1960, p. 68). He points to the potential for mental and emotional distress when he asserts that the unembodied self has a relationship 'with the body which can become very complex' (Laing 1960, p. 68). The unembodied self may 'long more than anything for participation in the world' yet it seeks to 'transcend the world and hence to be safe' (Laing 1960, p. 80).

A recent, very successful 'Heads Together' mental health campaign in the UK around the time of the Virgin London Marathon 2017 was aimed at raising awareness and encouraging discussion around mental health. On one of my social media feeds a friend who had watched the related BBC television documentary 'Mind Over Marathon' said that one of the runners for the charity asked if there was perhaps a nicer word than 'mental' to use, given the often derogatory and social associations attached to the word mental. What struck me, not for the first time, was why we need to separate out one part of our experience from the other at all. Of course, having language to try and accurately pinpoint what it is we are talking about is important, enabling people to have vocabulary to facilitate expression and to make sense of experience is central to psychotherapy. Exercise 5.1 helps facilitate understanding of the mind–body split.

Exercise 5.1 A holistic approach to distress

Complete this exercise with another person if possible. You may either write this down or speak about the subject.

1. Take a moment to think of a period of life where you have felt an enduring sense of depression or of low mood or have been particularly anxious.

2. Try and describe how you felt (or feel, if it is still present) during this period of time, without reference to your body or to any physical aspect.

▶

◄

3. What is missing from your description? How difficult or easy was it to make that distinction?

4. Next, reflect on a period of time that stands out for you where you have suffered from an enduring physical illness.

5. Now attempt to describe the physical illness without making reference to any aspect that might usually be considered in the mental, emotional or spiritual sphere.

6. Again, what is missing from your description? How difficult or easy was it to makes this distinction? How did your experience of this part of the exercise feel compared to step 3?

Why does the separation of the physical and mental matter?

To begin with, Exercise 5.2 helps us to see just how little sense it makes to try and focus on anything in either the physical or mental realm without reference to the other realm. The ramifications of the split are much more harmful than just an inability to articulate experience. Today, in Western society at least, we live in a world which approaches bodies as objects to be at various times manipulated, categorized, harmed, changed, and all too often to be cast as imperfect and shameful. We project onto bodies all kinds of meanings based on how they look, attributing moral qualities to shape, size, age, ill health and activity. There is an underlying assumption that our bodies need to be controlled and manipulated, that we cannot trust in our various appetites, if indeed we are aware of them at all.

The acceptable faces of objectification?

Perhaps the most obvious example of the level of objectification of our age is the 'selfie'. The rise of social media over the last decade has had a substantial impact on our day-to-day views of ourselves and how many of us live. It is difficult to walk through London without colliding with selfie sticks waving in the wind. For many, life is approached as a series of potential images of self to capture, filter, zoom in and out, manipulate and publish to the world. While this obviously provides fun and connection for many people, it is an extreme representation of just how far removed we are from privileging *experiencing* and how much we objectify our bodies as if we are external observers. Kanner and Gomes (1995, p. 82) wrote about 'The All-Consuming Self' before the age of social media. They described the creation of a consumer false self that they proposed as being born from 'a merciless distortion of authentic human needs and desires' (Kanner and Gomes, p. 83). In the context of discussions about consumerism and the environment, Kanner and Gomes also reflect on how children learn to substitute what they are told they want, in this case material possessions, for what they truly want so that a person's authentic needs, desires and experiences are so deeply buried that they cease to be aware of their presence or loss.

Too fat, too thin...

When I first started to write this chapter, it was the beginning of January and everywhere I seemed to look I saw a media saturated with diet, exercise and weight-loss adverts. Lose weight ... sleep more ... exercise more ... top 5 tips for a healthy...Better ... New ... you. Exercise and dieting supplements were falling out of the Sunday papers urging bodily transformation towards some supposed utopian ideal (in my house making their way swiftly to the recycling bin). There is nothing wrong with the overall aim of moving towards a healthy lifestyle and recognizing the importance of food and drink to our holistic health and wellbeing, yet these images contain so many other messages that are far from healthy and that are implicitly underpinned by the themes of both not being good enough and of being a detached observer. Related very closely to the coverage of food, appetite and body image is the way in which sex and sexuality is objectified. The aim of attaining the body beautiful is inextricably linked in to sex and desire, as if what is desirable is objective and non-relational. Sex and sexuality is also split off and assessed as if it is a separate entity from the rest of life.

In our present Western culture there are advantages to attempting to control and manage food intake, and many of the diets are well researched. Following them would certainly improve some people's quality of life. The issue, though, is the arbitrary nature with which they address wellbeing and the messages that they convey. They are guilty of objectifying our bodies and urging us to be out of touch with our bodily rhythms. The objectification and manipulation inherent in many of these messages leads to a sense of failure for many people, and for others has much more serious consequences, that will be discussed later.

The obsessive pursuit of the ideal body for whatever reason, through restrictive or modified eating, is at the same time accompanied by a hero worship of food and cooking and the idealization of chefs. Clients who present with eating disorders, or distressed eating, describe their obsession with food and eating. It would be understandable to see this as a trait of disorder or distress, a symptom in the conventional sense, and yet the obsessive worship of food is shared much more widely than just in people that might meet diagnostic criteria for eating disorders or that feel the need to seek psychotherapeutic help for their distress. On television we watch cooking shows in which celebrities compete to become chefs or endeavour to master the craft of designing elaborate cakes in baking competitions. At the same time, if we chose to, we could switch channels and watch evaluations of diet plans. Social media news streams are overwhelmed with pictures of flash, Photoshopped restaurant food plates while at the same time urging us to be thin and controlled and strive for the 'body beautiful'. Television viewers watch celebrity judges salivate over freshly cooked masterpieces, removing themselves from their own appetites. A common theme present in working with people in eating distress is people feeling that they do not know whether they are hungry or not, or if they do eat, when they should stop. They are disconnected from their own bodies and appetites, food and body becoming distanced in objectification. This is not just true of people with markedly distressed eating; it is endemic in Western society. Orbach (2000) describes her psychotherapy work with a client, Edgar, who had been eating for some time without awareness or knowledge of any hunger. One of the exercises that she asks Edgar to complete is to pay attention to what

Exercise 5.2 Hunger and appetite

Note the main occasions of eating in the last 24 hours. This can be adapted and expanded to include feelings around food and potential triggers, and to understand wider motivations, but the aim of this exercise is to explore how aware you (or your client) are of the physical needs of eating. This can form the basis of a more extended exploration.

Food eaten	What facilitated this	Aware of being hungry or not?	What ended this eating?

he eats to try and become aware of when he feels physically content, and therefore of the signal to stop eating (Orbach 2000, p. 119). Orbach suggests that this might sound simple to someone without an eating problem, though I also think that many of us feel quite similar to Edgar in our disassociation from our physical needs and appetites. Exercise 5.2 encourages reflection on how we approach our appetites and is particularly useful for people that feel disconnected from their bodily awareness.

Nourishing ourselves: nature hunger

When we consider appetite, our first image is usually that of sustaining ourselves through the food that we put into our body. Rust, a Jungian analyst and eco-psychologist, has spent many years working with people with difficult relationships with food and argues for widening the framework of what we think of as hunger and appetite to include the natural world. Rust suggests that we are all 'hungry for a relationship with land, with place, with our bodies. This is nature hunger' (Rust 2008, p. 77). She describes how 'spending time outside, whether it be in our back gardens or in the wilds of nature, is profoundly healing, and this can be a powerful ally in helping us to recover a relationship with our nature' (Rust 2008). In Michael Roads' accounts of his relationship in nature, he portrays the nourishment of his whole being which nature offered him. Rust's 'nature hunger' relates to the theme of disconnection from experience (Roads 1985).

Too painted, too aged ...

A central message of our time is that we can never be too young as adults. In the same way that the 'Nothing tastes as good as thin feels' indoctrination pervades much of media and advertising, the ideal is also to be implicitly as young as possible. Women in particular, though men increasingly so, are constantly judged on how they look in comparison to their actual age and encouraged to manipulate themselves to look like something that they are biologically not. It is the ultimate compliment of our age to say that a person looks younger than their biological age. Botox needles, dermal fillers and cosmetic surgeons' scalpels are becoming more and more routine, the norm in some environments, in order that the utopian dream of staying forever young can be relentlessly pursued. The denial of physical aging is what Sartre (2003) might term a constant act of social 'mauvais foi' (translated as 'bad faith') as swathes of people and cultural machinery act as if to deny aging. This is perhaps one of the ultimate expressions of objectifying our physical existence. We discussed earlier the collective environmental denial that has the implicit assumption that our planet will not change, and our approach to our own aging seems to contain similar traits.

Cut, starved, sexually assaulted...

What we have considered thus far relating to objectification and disconnection shows us the potential damage of distancing the physical. The extent of damage varies widely and can be seen on a continuum from mild to extremely severe distress. Clients come to psychotherapy with many deep troubles that relate to this whole area. People starve themselves, at times resulting in death, to manipulate their bodies, sometimes as an attempt to experience feeling in their body and sometimes the opposite. Either way there is an expression of a very difficult relationship in the physical dimension.

The sort of self-harm that involves scratching, cutting, burning, purging and starving obviously requires psychotherapeutic help. Yet this can also be considered in relationship to some of the behaviours and practices that are much more acceptable, indeed lauded in current Western society. Nips, tucks, injecting needles, shaving, waxing, tattooing, tanning, are all behaviours of doing something to the body object, with scant regard for the experience of the body. It is a rite of passage to explain to our daughters and sons that waxing is painful; magazines are full of articles telling us how to put up with the discomfort. Far better to conform to the de-forested ideal and experience pain than be comfortable as nature intended. This is not to suggest that these routine activities are comparable to the distress or risk of the sort of harm that we see in therapy, rather to encourage critical reflection on the status quo of the body object.

How might embodied disconnection present in the psychotherapy room?

It is tempting to automatically look to our clients' expression in psychotherapy and consider potential ways in which they might be disconnected from either their natural roots or feel disembodied. Before we focus on potential client experiences I think it is necessary first to go back to the fundamentals of therapy practice. Let us consider the construction of psychotherapy, the therapeutic relationship, the prevailing assumptions around the conceptualization of mental health diagnosis.

Psychotherapy construction and the therapeutic relationship

The majority of psychotherapy practice takes place indoors, already one step removed from the sensory experiences of the natural world. Psychotherapists often make attempts to bring in nature to the practice space: pictures of seascapes, of beautiful trees and forests, and bowls of tactile stones and perhaps driftwood ornaments serve other therapeutic and aesthetic purposes but they also are a small attempt to re-connect with the world 'out there'. In my first therapy training, as a neophyte practitioner, I was taught that the aim of the psychotherapy environment was to create a space as neutral as possible in order, I think, to remove as much bias of my own construction as possible. I might argue that one person's or culture's idea of neutral is another's meaning-laden bland hell, and throughout my training and teaching since then I have heard many joke-laden conversations about peach therapy rooms with 1990s soft-focus Athena prints. The construction of the therapeutic space is just one aspect of how we can encourage or discourage connection with our physical world, both in terms of the natural world and in terms with our physicality. For example, most adult psychotherapy is conducted sitting on chairs whereas in the majority of play therapy or work with younger children the physical environment becomes much more important with the younger client choosing to sit on the floor, for example. How would we feel asking our clients if they would like to sit outside on the grass bank, or go for a walk around the grounds of the institution in which we provide psychotherapy? What would this challenge in us around boundaries, our understanding of what psychotherapy is and is not? How do we feel sitting inside in our rooms for much of the day? Technological advancements mean that some of the more traditional boundaries have shifted for many of us as we offer remote access therapy. Perhaps this might ignite us to reconsider the benefits of shifting boundaries in other directions. In the following chapter we will consider the healing potential of natural environments in more detail.

Assumptions around the conceptualization of mental distress and diagnosis

To begin with, Exercise 5.3 helps to focus on the status quo of our focus in psychotherapy.

It is interesting to reflect on how often the primary focus of psychotherapy is on the personal or social aspects of existence, with the physical being assumed to be less relevant to any current distress. Equally the potential for the natural environment as a source of healing is too easily dismissed. When we have our initial assessment with clients we might ask 'How do you feel?', 'What is troubling you?'. It is my experience in teaching and training that the physicality of distress is overlooked. What awareness might unfold if we increase our focus on questions such as '*Where* do you feel sad, or happy or anxious'? Expanding the traditional focus, such as that outlined in DSM V (American Psychiatric Association (APA) 2013), gives us potential for greater insight into the make-up of our clients' lived experience and more completely and holistically locates their distress *in the world*.

Exercise 5.3 What factors matter

Spend five minutes imagining your first session with a new client; if you are already practising it is helpful to consider an actual person that you have worked with recently. If you are not practising, try and think about what you would think important to ask. In the space below write down a list of the main questions that you asked your client:

▶

◀

Divide these questions into four groups. It might be that you have none in one category and many in another.

Physical   Social   Personal   Spiritual

Turning to nature to feel embodied and connected

Being grounded and embodied in nature

The sort of experiences of immersion in nature that are outlined by Brazier (2011) and Roszak (Roszak et al. 1995) point to the increased awareness and sense of expansion of embodied feelings taking prominence over intellectual and verbal understandings. Mainstream therapy tends to focus on words and dialogue. In contrast, being in nature helps people to focus on the preverbal and experiential, and frees up experience, especially for those that might feel stuck in particularly narratives (Brazier 2011). Part of what it means to feeling embodied, grounded and connected is a feeling of being 'at home' in nature, rooted to earth, returning to something fundamental and essential, awakening to a feeling that we are intrinsically linked to and a part of a natural world (Jordan 2009a). This feeling of being embodied and having a place was captured evocatively by Conran when he wrote 'Each blade of grass has its spot on earth whence it draws its life, its strength; and so is man rooted to the land from which he draws his together with his life' (Conran 1900, p. 167).

Shifting sensory focus

In the accounts of research participants (Macgregor 2013), the tactile, sensual, physical experience of being in nature was described as the epitome of life by those people that had experienced varying kinds of transformation through immersion in the natural world. These sensory experiences were described as being extremely absorbing, encouraging a focus on being present rather than on thinking, planning and achieving, and a focus on experience rather than on being able to articulate or understand. As one participant articulated 'And just drinking it all in ... taking it all in without any expectation, any kind of judgement or, you know, any need to kind of ... mould or design the moment ... or control it. It was just like ... What more can you do?' (Macgregor 2013).

Nature's transformation: experiencing being embodied

A greater awareness of being embodied in nature is described as being particularly important by those people that describe themselves as often relying on their intellectual functioning or 'being in their head' (Macgregor 2013). Feeling greater embodiment is likened to feeling grounded. The sensory connection of being in nature is part of this feeling: wind blowing on the face, being open to the warmth, cold, wet and dry is a personal reminder of human embodiment. Something of the feeling of being embodied that is experienced increases a more holistic appreciation and awareness of self. This seems to facilitate a more nurturing, caring and accepting attitude to self and body. Increased embodied awareness is transformative in relation to body image; feeling experience in the body rather than judging it from outside seems to facilitate more acceptance of physicality and what might more usually be judged as imperfection.

Part of feeling greater embodiment facilitates an increased sense of head, heart and body coming together, less of a sense of the split that we talked about earlier between different facets of our being. This sense of holistic self is linked also to feeling a greater connection as part of nature. Sometimes going outdoors into nature seems to be a deliberate movement towards confronting holistic embodied experience, facing an expanded reality that is sometimes hidden below or behind social constructs.

Bodily knowing

During the interviews for my research, one participant described experiencing *a bodily knowing* that does not require or focus on intellectual understanding, and this is also talked about in a similar vein as being in touch with a more authentic knowledge. Through being in nature there is potential to help clients (and ourselves) expand our understanding. Part of the shift towards focusing on the body is an increased awareness of what *feels* right when facing life choices and of being able to hold contradictions and uncertainty. In one of my personal experiences of feeling completely connected in nature, I described feeling a movement towards valuing self experience and feeling that being in nature helps rebalance more authentic being, as opposed to the more usual attitude of trying to fit in with social norms. Being in nature increases self-acceptance, as outlined in the following excerpt: 'There's a bigger life going on. And then I suppose looking at that heron, or swimming through that green water, just ... there's another side to it. And it reminds me also that there's another side to me' (Macgregor 2013).

Opening ourselves to the sensory vitality of being in nature shifts us towards emotional relating and away from verbal understandings. This stands in contrast to many of the assumptions of therapy practice, particularly that verbal and cognitive understanding is facilitative and emotionally helpful.

Linette's wild swimming

Linette lives in the city and has found a pond with ducks on it that she described as her 'little gap to nature'. When we met, she was taking weekly retreats to the pond and she talked about how these retreats helped her to not get too caught up in things. Linette's routine was to dive into the pond and swim 100 metres to the far bank. She described one experience where, on the other side, there was a heron nesting and she floated there for a little while, looking at the heron and watching him make his nest. As she watched she felt calm and present. She saw him taking little straws and pieces of twigs and building his home. Linette feels that she always has a pile of things to do waiting for her, and that if she just goes there once a week to touch base, it acts as a reminder that there's a bigger life out there. As she looked at the heron, and as she swam through the green water she saw life happening in a way that was very different from her day-to-day work and living. Seeing this 'other side' reminds her also that there's another side to herself. Often Linette feels like a failure, and this experience shows her another side to herself – a side that likes swimming, that appreciates these moments, that is playful and calm.

Linette relished the very physical experience of jumping into freezing water, which contrasted with her more intellectual day-to-day focus. She feels more completely alive, grounded in the coldness of the experience. Linette described how, when she gets out of the water, she does not want to take a shower, instead wanting to hold the experience a little bit longer on her skin. Physically she is very tired and part of this experience leads her to a more holistic awareness.

Linette spoke of her retreats into nature as private 'no strings attached' moments where she exists at her own pace and by her rules. She described how important this is to her, particularly because she feels she often plays by other people's rules. There was a sense that her outside swimming helps shake up her self-perception and her usual view of her strengths and weaknesses. She feels more able to be with and accept her own rhythm and pace; indeed to enjoy and luxuriate in it. Linette finds the experience liberating and fun; she describes how this creeps into her wider life and relationships, making her feel more playful.

Linette experiences a real connection through being aware of the seasons: that nature provides reassurance through the combination of its continued presence and the knowledge that the seasons are in a process of continuous change. She talked about how she goes through coldness but then through being warm again, so that in the depths of the chill of winter there is knowledge and reassurance of spring and summer. Linette takes something of the cycle into her day-to-day life. If she is experiencing 'a down', it's ultimately alright because the season will change again and she will end up in a warmer season, or the hope of a spring season. This is very reassuring and helps Linette approach life and her own experience more fluidly. A couple of years ago she went through a very low spell in which her appreciation of nature helped put into a particular perspective. Rather than describe this as depression, she talked about her 'bit of winter'. She said that she knows that if, or when, winter comes again, she will know that after winter comes spring or summer. This awareness or the transitory nature of each moment eases the tension of trying to escape something or trying to get away from a particular feeling or experience.

When Linette is in nature and has a significant moment she feels completely peaceful. She said that this is not really a euphoria; it is not a major inspirational feeling, rather it feels more like a sense of calmness, a feeling of contentment. For Linette, this calmness and contentment is much more important that euphoria or inspiration.

When Linette looks at the dark clouds outside of her window she sees them passing, and this is reassuring in terms of how she perceives herself. If she thinks about nature it reminds her of how she sees herself. At one moment there are dark clouds and at the same time there might be glimpses of beautiful, lighter clouds. There will be dark clouds, but Linette suggested that if she looks enough, or waits, there will be blue sky as well.

Linette also talked about going swimming in the Mediterranean. She recalled looking down at the teal water, a colour she has always loved, and how she realized that there were so many shades, that nature offered a vastness that is almost incomprehensible and cannot be covered by the limitations of language. This experience connected with her, making her aware that she cannot just pigeonhole herself or pigeonhole other things. This widens her outlook on life, as she realizes that there is so much more that she cannot begin to imagine and that she does not know about and need not categorize.

As well as feeling that she needs to be mindful of nature's vastness, Linette appreciates that the natural world is made out of small atoms, so she feels it is important to value the details as well. She used the analogy of Monet's painting of water lilies to show the connectedness she feels in nature between the smallest atoms being part of the vast whole. Nature shows her that she has to value both zoning in and zoning out and that this is how she lives her life. Linette feels that she has to zone in to make her experience in the world, as part of the vast, complex system, worthwhile.

Linette feels a connectedness from each of the small things of her day-to-day life and the vastness of nature as the planet goes around. This sense of nature being infinitely big and at the same time incomprehensibly small feels spiritual to Linette, even supernatural. She feels that she is trying to make something with her time on this planet and that she feels that she might as well do it with something she likes or something she thinks will contribute in some way or make her happy. That through the ultimate connectedness, her being happy or content will spill out into the system. Being part of this vast system provides some liberation for her: the world will go ahead no matter what she does, and she takes the idea that 'it's not the end of the world' very literally. She feels that it does not really matter what she does here, or if she struggles to make a decision; is does not even matter which decision she makes since it is hardly going to influence the seasons or the world.

Linette talked to me about how she feels that nature gives her hints about how to live life in a way that she does not get outside of nature. Nature helps Linette see the bigger picture; it is calming and helps her feel a connected part of something bigger. The transformative experiences that Linette has in nature are moments that she cannot force: if she looks for a particular experience in nature sometimes she is frustrated that she cannot find it. She waits for nature to radiate to her, maintaining an openness and an awareness to the connection. An over-riding theme of Linette's is how she takes nature's metaphors into her everyday life. Natural evolution and transformation reassure Linette that as the seasons change, so difficult times in life are not permanent. When Linette does not have connection to nature she notices changes: if she has been too long in the city she feels a sense of gloominess and a stuck-ness of being in her head for too long. This sensation is a feeling of being trapped in a closed circular system with thoughts going round and round in a rather disconnected and repetitive motion.

The hints that nature shows Linette are much more than a faith; they are the picture of the world, a truth rather than a metaphor or analogy, since she is part of the nature that she observes. Linette turns to nature for guidance, looking to what she feels part of. To some extent this feels like she is turning to a truth in herself. This is not a searching for an experience, it is as if the natural world shows her something of herself, holding a reflective mirror.

Implications for practice

1. In the Western world, we live in an age where we routinely feel disconnected from our bodies. Acknowledging that as the status quo for many people allows us to help our clients gain awareness.

2. The split of inner life from outer world is relatively recent. Currently these views (of connection, of viewing us as part of a greater whole) might seem 'alternative' or uncomfortable, but they are part of an enduring wisdom of ancient societies.

Expanding our therapeutic exploration to consider wider context may help clients feel less disconnected and isolated.

3. If we behave as if the natural world is of no consequence to our being we risk giving ourselves the same message about our own being. When we help clients face the choices that they are making we should bear in mind all of the dimensions of existence.

4. Help clients consider the day-to-day routine of their lives. How are they working with or against their bodies and their own appetites? How do they value their appetites in comparison to the messages that they receive from external sources?

5. Encourage reflection on the 'body-object'. What messages is the client giving to themselves?

6. Consider the make-up of the therapy space. Bring nature into the room or take the room outside, where safe and practical.

6

The Nature of Healing

And the old people liked to remove their moccasins and walk with bare feet on the sacred earth ... and it was the final abiding place of all things that lived and grew. The soil was soothing, strengthening, cleansing and healing...

Luther Standing Bear (accessed 2018)

Human beings have turned to nature for emotional and spiritual healing across cultures and time and this chapter will begin with a journey through rituals and practices in order to demonstrate the power of being in nature and its impact on psychological and spiritual healing. Drawing on the writings of Emerson (1849), Hillman (1995) and Roszak et al. (1995) we will consider how focusing on being a part of the natural world enables us to begin to transform our approach to both our own mental and emotional healing and potentially that of the planet in which we exist. Running throughout eco-therapy literature and therapeutic practice is the central idea that we cannot maintain health as individual human beings if we are part of an unhealthy system. This obviously implies that as we consider the nature of healing, we endeavour to take a more holistic stance and embrace the idea that health or ill health is predicated on the wellbeing and resilience of the wider environment. Orr, writing in the foreword to Buzzell and Chalquist (2009), says 'We now know, however, that the health of any living system is seldom tied to any single part but is dependent on both lesser and larger things. In other words, health is a systems concept that cannot be split off from the whole' (Buzzell and Chalquist 2009, p. 13).

Addressing the split

It is only rather recently that we have assumed a nature/human separation as being the norm. Hillman asks us to reflect on whether human beings have been so divorced from the spirit of their surroundings at any other time in history (Hillman 1995, p. xxii). Bateson proposes a more caring, integrated approach to nature, suggesting that an 'I–Thou relationship is conceivable between man and his society or ecosystem' (Bateson 1972, p. 452). This sort of attitude to relationship, where love and care are privileged over purpose and function, offers the potential for a much deeper emotional experience with nature. Eco-psychologists and eco-therapists propose that we need to address the problem of our alienation from nature in order to live a meaningful, fulfilling life (Clinebell 1996). In a similar vein, Snyder described the feeling of connection as being like a fulfilling reunion, finding a whole again (Snyder 1989, p. 172). Other eco-therapists, such as Kanner and Gomes, commonly report dramatic breakthroughs and feelings of awakening to a much wider experience of being when working with people on trips into the wilderness (Kanner and Gomes 1995, p. 91). They detail how being in the natural world 'awakens in every fiber of our being the primal knowledge of connection and graces us with a few moments of sheer awe, it can shatter the hubris and isolation so necessary of narcissistic defences' (Kanner and Gomes 1995, p. 91).

The writings of Carl Jung continue to influence much of the eco-psychology movement and show the deep connection and wholeness that Jung experienced being in nature (Jung 1967). Jung spent extended periods of time immersed in nature at his retreat in Bollingen on the edge of Lake Zurich and travelled extensively around the world. When Jung was travelling in New Mexico he had a dialogue with a Pueblo Indian at the foot of some mountains. Jung described realizing that all life came from the mountain and its water: 'I felt a swelling emotion connected with the word "mountain"' (Jung 1967, p. 249). He suggested that if we 'put away all European rationalism ... If we set aside our intimate knowledge of the world and exchange it for a horizon that seems immeasurable' we will have an 'inner comprehension' that 'all life comes from the mountain' (Jung 1967, p. 249). This transformative, experiential understanding connects with something outside of what we normally see as our own boundaries: 'At times I feel like I am spread out over the landscape and inside things' (Jung 1967, p. 252).

People have been spending time in wild nature to facilitate emotional healing and spiritual awakening for centuries: more formal wilderness therapy practices are recent modifications of age-old endeavours. Through exploring some of these practices, ancient and modern, we will consider the profound potential of being in wild nature and look at how we might tailor some of the underlying concepts of extended excursions into wilderness into our more everyday lives.

Being in nature has shown to be intensively healing for people that have experienced severe trauma and torture in the most harrowing of circumstances. Linden and Grut (2002) pioneered therapeutic work using nature and gardening as sanctuary for people that have been badly emotionally and mentally scarred. What practices might be considered to help clients in their path to emotional and psychological healing and how might we use nature to heal and sustain ourselves? Connecting with the cycles of the natural world has the potential to help us make sense of the dilemmas and distresses of living. In research on transformative experiences in nature, being in nature was experienced as emotionally healing and transformative and I will include some of the key themes that arose from that research in this chapter (Macgregor 2013).

Nature and healing

We often hear people say that being in nature is good for us, and I am supposing that you would not be engaged with this writing if you did not share something of this position. We tend to associate being in nature with inhaling clean, fresh air (though of course this is often not the case), perhaps with taking part in healthy exercise, a lung-busting hill walk, a cycle along the banks of a river, tiring out children with a run around the park. The potential healing benefits that immediately spring to mind are associated with the physical side of health, wellbeing and healing. I suspect that most people would not have that much difficulty grappling with the concept of engaging in activities in the great outdoors being linked to physical healing. Perhaps because of the engrained physical/mental split that underpins much of modern day approaches to overall wellbeing, it seems to be a far greater stretch of our imaginations and prejudices to consider that we might turn to nature for our own and others' emotional and psychological healing. Yet it is widely documented that when people are out in nature, spending time walking, for example, or in environmental restoration projects or wilderness retreats they feel broadly better about themselves in a much more holistic sense than just a physical one. However, it remains difficult to unravel what this means, what is going on, and any idea that being in nature actually heals is assumed to be a bit wacky or somewhat alternative. Later in this chapter we will see how it was not always thus and we will reflect on how indigenous peoples across different continents and different ages have had mental and spiritual healing embedded in their daily routines and customs. Harper, a wilderness practitioner, reminds us that 'people have always turned to wilderness to become whole again' (Harper 1995, p. 184). Approximately 2,500 years ago Hippocrates (2009 [nd]) wrote in his treatise 'On Airs, Waters and Places' that to consider the health of any person we must examine very carefully the environment and seasons of that person.

Deurzen describes the impact of time spent in nature in more familiar activities than specific therapy wilderness experiences. 'Immersion in nature (walking, gardening, sailing etc.) has tremendously positive effects on all human functioning' (Deurzen 2008, p. 54). Higley and Milton (2008) have found that even brief contact with the natural world provides relief from stress and that 'there are also longer term, more profound benefits to be gained through contact with the natural world' (Higley and Milton 2008: 36). Hicks, a chartered counselling psychologist, concurs: 'I think it can have important implications for our sense of self experiencing a true connection with the world around us' (Hicks 2008, p. 7). Research commissioned by Mind (2007) shows that individual mental health improves substantially after being in nature: 94% of those surveyed highlighted a range of mental health benefits in relation to 'green' exercise when compared to similar physical exercise in non-green environments (Mind 2007, p. 20). Even in our technologically focused, individualist age, people across disciplines do acknowledge that our situational context and the world in which we live and breathe has rich potential for healing. Exercise 6.1 will help focus on our present experience with the nature and how we view the natural world. As in any other relationship, it is only through becoming honestly and openly aware of the present experience that we are able to consider whether or not change, development or nurturing might be beneficial.

Exercise 6.1 A nature–self audit

Consider the time that you spend outside or actively engaging with the natural world. Is being in nature part of your daily life or weekly routine, or are you rather more divorced from the natural world? If we take on board some of the ideas that we covered in the discussion about the quality of experience, we remind ourselves that attitude and intention are as important as quantity of experience. I have filled in two different personal examples as a starting point; one for myself and one from my daughter. Once you have made notes of your thoughts, begin to consider how you might improve the connection.

Activity	Feelings at the time	Attitude towards nature at the time	Thoughts and feelings now about the experience	Ideas for improving relationship
Walking the dog in torrential rain	In a rush, trying to do too much so disconnected from surroundings to begin with	Low awareness or thought and irritation with the rain	Feel guilty that I take these experiences for granted. I've often loved walking in the rain. Beginning to re-connect with environmental concerns. Thinking about why I have become disconnected	Re-connect with environmental concerns

▶

Orienteering in the woods	A bit bored to begin with, but slowly felt more confident and happy	A strong sense of freedom and independence. Really noticed the difference between light and shade	Really appreciative	Make time for similar experiences, not just when organized by other people

Rituals and practices – ancient and modern

Ancient practices, such as the healing-circle ceremonies of Native Americans, were based on the premise that being in nature has the potential for holistic healing (Metzner 1999). Winter and Koger (2010) described how being in wild nature has positive effects including experiencing 'positive emotions such as pleasure, happiness, satisfaction, peace and tranquillity' (Winter and Koger 2010, p. 254). However, there is a caution that runs throughout much of the eco-psychology writing against concerning *using* nature for healing since it is considered exploitative and human-centric (Greenway 1995; Winter and Koger 2010). Therefore, to think appropriately about healing, we need to begin to try and broaden our self- or individual-focused perspective.

Macy and Brown (1998) described in detail practices that might help us begin to heal our relationship with the world from a much more environmental stance. In pointing to the obvious environmental damage of our present age, they suggested that if we switch off from the pain that the world is feeling we necessarily switch off or deaden ourselves. In re-connecting with what is happening in the world, we re-connect with the pain and despair in the world, yet we also reawaken from what is described as a deadened, coma-like existence. Macy and Brown use terms found in psychoanalytic sources, such as denial and repression, in order to frame our present relationship with nature (Macy and Brown 1998). However, the denial and repression they speak of is a pain experienced or expressed by the individual but importantly located in the holistic system.

Foster and Little (1987) describe the re-creation of an ancient rite of passage of rebirth, called Vision Quest, based around a period of fasting in the wilderness in order to formally mark the end of a crisis, for example, and move over a threshold into a new way of being. A vision quest is a rite of passage of some native American people consisting of a series of ceremonies, usually undertaken alone, at sacred places in nature. Little describes how nature touched him: 'I saw that my journey would be an inward one, into the wilderness of my heart, and double-edged outward journey, into the wilderness of rock, sand, and water, and into the wild, tangled jungle of other people's lives. These wildernesses, so dissimilar, yet of the same Source, were bridged, connected, and made one, when I drew water from the rock' (Foster and Little 1987, p. 14).

Vision quest and holistic healing

Descriptions of Vision Quest experiences highlight beautifully an approach to living that truly considers experience as a whole, rather than the disparate parts that we extract from existence in modern-day Western healthcare, and more broadly throughout society. For example, spiritual practices are based on nurture from the physicality of the earth, enlightenment from actively and consciously experiencing being part of connected, embodied nature. I had the privilege of visiting the National Museum of the American Indian in Washington DC in the spring of 2017, while I was researching this book. As I immersed myself in the contents of the amazing structure I had hopeful senses sharply on the lookout for experiences specifically related to an ancient approach to emotional and mental health. My quest was somewhat in vain and rather misguided. What I experienced was an integrated exposition of what it means to live well, to heal, to commune. Politics, emotionality, community, spirituality, poetry, food all integrated and inter-dependent. It was impossible to dissect and delineate in the way that Western medicine is accustomed to. To extract any specific focus from the whole would be to diminish understanding to such an extent that meaning shifts.

A Cree Indian, named Walk Sacred, describes the holistic experience of taking part in a Vision Quest in nature: 'As each day goes by, the phases of life go through their cycles. At night, the stars come out. Pleiades will actually dance for you if you're a vision quester. They light up, almost like a neon sign. I know people find that hard to believe, but that's just the mystery of the ceremony. An eagle will hover right over you knowing that you're in ceremony. Thunder and lightning come by, and you just endure it. It's no problem. Lightning can be flashing all around you, and you'll laugh. The Great Spirit is not going to take your life up there while you are vision questing. And if it does, who cares? You're in a good state. But you don't fear nature or God. The Great Spirit made you. Why should you fear it? You become more confident once you follow this natural road' (Native American Indians 2011).

The Medicine Wheel

Foster and Little (1999) based what they defined as 'four shields' psychology on the medicine wheel of Native American tradition, where the four directions correspond with compass points, the seasons and psychological stages. The Medicine Wheel is based on the belief that happiness and wellbeing is produced not on external conditions or circumstances but on our thoughts and responses to our lived experience (Native American Indians 2011).

The Medicine Wheel played a significant part in moving towards the long truce that followed hundreds of years of native American tribes being at war with each other. A great Iroquois chief, who became Hiawatha, formed an alliance that would later become the Confederation of Nations. The alliance focused on the similarities between Indian peoples, rather than on the differences that had for such a long time been the source of great tension and war. Located in the Bighorn National Forest, the Medicine Wheel is approximately 75 feet in diameter and is a circular rock circle with a cairn of stones in the middle. It was constructed between 300 and 800 years ago and prayer offerings are still left at the wheel today. Practices at the wheel focused on strengths and weaknesses and helped people concentrate on areas of personal growth. The wheel is made up of four directions: north, east, south and west. Each person is represented somewhere in the circle with individual placements being associated with a moon, animal power, mineral, or colour, for example (Native American Indians 2011). It was mandatory for people to work on themselves as part of the collective or else risk leaving the tribal community. After many generations, the focus had shifted away from blame and anger, as had been the focus in the years of tribal wars, to the extent that these concepts seemed alien. In Chapter 6 we will use ideas from the medicine wheel in exploring self-awareness and identity. The exercise that follows (Exercise 6.2) uses the ideas behind the formation of the alliance all those years ago to help challenge and reframe difficult experience.

Exercise 6.2 Shifting focus and taking responsibility (in pairs or individually) – using nature as an example

This exercise can work powerfully in supervision as well as in relational therapy or individual awareness.

There is an old saying, particularly popular with outdoor enthusiasts, that there is no such thing as bad weather, simply bad clothing or equipment. My perspective on weather shifts according to my expectations, desires and habits. I might be angry that it rained all day and ruined my plans for a long run, a picnic or whatever. Alternatively, I might be grateful for cooling rain after weeks of sun,

▶

◄

grateful for the restorative power of the rain on my dried out garden. I might be both angry and grateful, or whatever: what matters is that these feelings are not *caused* by the rain but by my wider context, attitude or intention. What *is* important is recognizing my responsibility for my own attitude – privileging certain feelings and/or thoughts over others.

Begin by imagining a recent situation in which you felt angry with another person about something that (you perceived) they had done. Spend a few minutes remembering the incident.

1. Retell the incident, either by writing it down or by narrating it, if you have the opportunity to complete this exercise with somebody else. In your description, be as honest as possible. Once you have given an agreed amount of time (say 5 minutes) to the initial description, stop. If you have not yet written it down, spend another couple of minutes making notes of the key points that you raised. Then focus on the following questions:

   - Did you apportion blame for the experience?

   - Did you apportion blame for your feelings ('He made me so angry' 'She's just so selfish').

   - In your retelling of the incident and in your notes, did you focus on the experience or the individuals in it, or a combination of both?

2. Return to the situation and try and retell it as 'factually' as possible, paying particularly attention to the language used and to whenever you make an automatic link between someone doing something, or an incident, and your emotional response to it. If you are completing this in pairs, as one person retells the situation the other should listen out and sensitively challenge bias and judgement, wherever possible and appropriate.

Now consider what other emotional responses there might be to the situation (trying to take yourself out of a feeling of what might feel like an automatic reaction). Can you consider the whole situation, moving from your own perspective? Next focus on describing the personal qualities of both you and the other person. Try and be as generous as possible. Spend some time thinking about what you value in the relationship with the other person. When you have really explored this move to the final retelling.

3. Retell the story a final time, paying attention to the shared experience, to the context and to focusing on description as opposed to explanation or judgement.

4. Compare the original version with the last retelling. What stands out for you?

Nature's impact on emotional, cognitive and spiritual healing

When I was exploring transformative experiences in nature I was particularly interested in focusing on the detail of people's encounters. In this section I will focus on some key themes related to healing that came to light:

– Emotional healing and increasing emotional resilience

– Coping with uncertainty and contradictions

– Feeling alive in the midst of pain

– Shifting perspective

– Helping with physical pain

– Healing without words.

Being in nature has also been shown to have a healing impact on people that are grieving and on helping heal people that have been through traumatic experiences.

Increasing emotional acceptance and resilience – stillness and peace

People describing transformative experiences in nature have a feeling of being very present in time which encourages a feeling of stillness and peace, present even in the midst of descriptions of very painful emotional experiences of grief and loss. Nature seems to help balance emotional experiences and people feel able to accept their experience *as it is*. Something about being in nature allows people to soften ideas of what is or is not appropriate emotional experience or expression, and perhaps also to loosen the meaning constructs that might be attached to particular emotions.

There is something of a transcendental quality to emotional healing. Nature seems to heal in a way that feels difficult to articulate and/or rationally understand. Being in nature also seems to foster a general sense of emotional resilience which seems related to feelings of connection, of not being alone, of being able to face uncertainty, and more fluid boundaries and of changing perspectives around what is important. Being more aware of and accepting of present experience helps connection with painful experiences of loss and sadness which are often distanced in our day-to-day lives. Although being in touch with these experiences is painful, there seems to be a relief and liberation from allowing experiences to arise, rather than being repressed or thwarted, and to be considered as more integrated in broader holistic experience. Roads describes healing in nature as 'allowing a powerful inner reality to emerge' (Roads 1985, p. 42). Being in touch with these sorts of feelings helps facilitate being able to make sense of experiences and linked to an increase sense of being alive, even during times of physical and emotional pain.

Being in nature is experienced as calming and facilitates a greater sense of contentment, peace and comfort, as well as a feeling of stillness. Solace and calm are found spending time in woods, in oceans of wheat fields, on beaches, at the tops of mountains, and nature seems to draw people towards such experiences.

Anxiety seems to dissipate in the feeling of being present; partly this is correlated with letting go of social norms and partly it is noted that moving in nature seems to help alleviate anxious feelings. Once anxiety becomes less of a focus or central emotional feature, other emotions are allowed to surface and there is a sense of being in touch with what is emotionally more meaningful, regardless of whether this is pleasant or distressing. To this extent being in nature is emotionally healing in that it facilitates awareness and expression of emotional experience as it arises.

Coping with uncertainty and contradictions

Certainty is less valued in nature, by contrast to day-to-day life which values drawing distinctions. Being with diffuseness, subtlety and non-understanding becomes more acceptable. This is part of the experience of feeling more aware of the present and more embracing of fluid existence, of being in each moment as opposed to focusing on more abstract ideas of what matters or how meaning is constructed.

Feeling alive in the midst of pain

The sensory and aesthetic wonder of being in nature facilitates a sense of aliveness in the midst of deep pain and turmoil. One research participant felt that focusing on the present helped open his heart after traumatic experiences that had felt desperate; this felt like slowly beginning to live again and part of a process of coming to terms with experience (Macgregor 2013). This is linked to both the relaxing of ideas of what is right or wrong as well as a more embracing acceptance of *whatever is there in present experience.*

Quality of emotional experience in nature

Ideas of what is appropriate emotional experience and expression seem less relevant in nature than everyday life. Research participants that I spoke to talked of how, in nature, they were able to express themselves emotionally as they experienced their feelings, rather than trying not to emote through holding back. Emotional experience also feels much nearer the surface, tears flow more easily, and this is accepted and valued. Emotions are felt and expressed in a more bodily way, without having to make sense first. In experience of fresh grief, sadness was felt in a deeper and different way than had previously been experienced. Returning on a daily basis into wild nature helped emotional expression during the experience of grief. Witnessing the rhythm and constant flow of nature helped make sense of the sadness and loss of grief, enabling the strength of feelings to be understood and, over time, accepted. This corresponds with other experiences where emotions held in the body seem to be loosened, freed up or unlocked, as if detaching from social meanings, norms and practices, notions of correct or appropriate behaviour and conventional understandings.

Shifting perspective on depressive experience

Nature provides a powerful metaphor that helps put the feeling of being depressed into context. For example, looking to the dark clouds and watching them pass over helps situate unhappy times in a wider prism of experience, providing reassurance and comfort. The sun will follow the clouds as spring follows winter. And there will be cloud again and winter again too. Being part of the cycle of life helps guard against feeling stuck in a particular experience. This also helps acceptance of other difficult aspects of life, such as what are sometimes viewed as personal traits. Seeing the world holistically as part of a system fosters a more fluid attitude. At the most difficult times in life, in profound devastation, nature helped depression and despair, providing solace and moments of peace. Being in nature was described as a being like a glimmer of hope in the darkest of nights (Macgregor 2013).

Physical pain in nature

Being in nature changed the experience of bodily pain, experienced as part of chronic physical health issues. Just being outside seems to ease pain and increase energy levels: this was noted even being still in nature, without the exercise benefits of increased endorphin levels. Part of the experience of having pain in nature is that physical pain leads to a more inward focus, whereas when a person is in less pain they feel more outwardly focused and appreciative of wider surroundings. For one participant in physical pain, she was drawn to the particular place that she was in while she was in pain. Knowing that she was in pain as she chose where to sit, she felt accepting of her experience as part of the whole of being in nature, just as she valued the rain and the sun as part of the weather system. This experience links back to the shift in perspective that happens as the focus moves from self to awareness of being part of the system.

Going into the garden was described by one person that I interviewed as being akin to a mini retreat, likened to being a 'nature bath' in terms of its relaxing quality (Macgregor 2013). One participant talked of feeling physically renewed in nature and that he felt sustained by nature sitting in the woods: connecting back to the importance of a particular quality of place, of place being central to the experience. There was a powerful description of nature as mother, offering the reassurance and comfort of being cradled and held. The experience of a renewed feeling of being embodied is part of the sense of renewal in being re-connected with experience not normally part of awareness.

Healing in nature for Alana

Alana's relationship to nature is central to her wellbeing: she has known this at a very embodied level for a long time. Alana took part in a 12-hour immersion in nature which she experienced as transformative: silent and alone for the duration. This immersion took place in a remote, exposed landscape on the Scottish mainland with amazing, expansive views out to sea and across to spectacular mountains. Throughout this time, although she was in physical pain as a result of long-term chronic health issues, Alana felt mentally and emotionally strong.

Alana's relationship with nature stretches back as far as she can remember, and she recalls in detail that when she was of primary school age she would cross over the road and she would be on the marshes, looking at curlews as she rode on the bus to school. Her primary school looked out over the water to Scotland and she would take part in field trips down on the shore.

Throughout the immersion experience that Alana took part in, she was in physical pain because of a chronic health condition. Alana noticed that when she was in less pain she was aware of looking outwards and enjoying what was going on around her. Even in her pain, it felt important to her to stay and experience, as if she was drawn to where she sat.

Alana chose her particular place for the immersions experience and felt that she had chosen a place that was completely right for her – she did not want for or long for what was not present; she felt content and at home. Sitting on the shore enabled her to look forward across the sea to the island mountains; turning behind she could see the lodge from where she had come. The landscape seems like a pivot on which she was poised between stillness and movement – stillness from being still on land looking towards the enduring presence of the mountains and movement from the sea and the weather and the passing of time.

Listening to the rain fall on the tarpaulin was a very beautiful experience, particularly in contrast to the more usual and every-day view of rain being a hindrance. Looking out to sea and seeing many rainbows was important – there seemed something symbolic in the rainbow's representation of the contrast between sun and rain, and Alana loved and valued this contrast. Being able to stick with and find the positive in the low points as well as the high points of both her felt physical embodied experience as well as the experience of the fluctuating elements was important for Alana. The transition moments between what Alana observed as the lows and the highs brought much beauty for her. When the sun came out after the rain she felt a real sense of joy and lightness in its warmth. Alana felt like a bird stretching out and expanding after being huddled up and cocooned. Both the expansive experience of looking out to the sea and the mountains as well as the tiniest detail of blades of grass moving and raindrops hitting the water were points of focus. Thinking about being in the mountains made Alana feel happy and she felt that her body wanted to relax just talking about it – she continues to experience a sense of peace and contentment on an ongoing basis when she thinks about or tunes into this experience. Being in nature is calming, relaxing, and she feels contented. This lightness feels freeing – Alana's face lights up and she smiles as she talks.

Being in nature grounds and helps centre Alana, and helps her rebalance her experience. Facets of life that matter seem clearer while peripheral concerns seem to fade away. The complications of everyday life are stripped back in nature to reveal a clear simplicity.

Alana experiences a sense of loss and sadness by the sea that touches her core. Alana feels that since she was a child she has had a real 'in the stomach' sense of sadness and loss. There is almost an element of yearning in it. This sadness is a sense of wanting something but not really knowing what that something is. Exist-ence feels simpler and slower in nature as Alana connects with what really matters in her life – a sense of what matters being revealed or announcing itself as unimportant things fade away evokes a present peace.

When Alana is near water, the sea in particular, she has a sense that she does not exist anymore. The feeling of sadness and loss that is familiar to her when she is near the sea is seen by her as relating to a feeling of her 'self' disappearing: that she is letting go of her ego in the experience of being 'part of' the landscape and nature. In nature, Alana feels that she knows who she is; that she returns to some truth about herself that is outside of a sense of 'ego' – a constructed sense of who she is that dissolves, particularly by the sea. Letting go of this is sad yet seems inevitable and is also a highly valued process.

Alana has a bodily knowing that she is part of the whole that is nature. This bodily knowing does not need intellectual understanding. At the beginning of her transformative experience, Alana was reflecting on the question 'who am I?'. She had a powerful experience that she was 'just this person sitting on this rock here, looking at those mountains over there – that's it, you don't need to know anything else'.

Alana feels that the interconnection that she experiences is spiritual – that she is linked to something much bigger. Alana is determined to hold and maintain the experiential awareness gained from her transformative experience in nature, particularly in terms of focusing on being more present with what is actually around her at each particular moment. Alana felt that she could not completely or adequately capture her transformative experiences or her relationship with nature in its entirety, and felt frustrated trying to share it with other people. Alana hopes that other people will experience it for themselves.

Nature and trauma

The healing power of nature is particularly relevant to people that have experienced profound trauma. Varying approaches to horticultural therapy are practised with a wide range of people from the projects run as part of EcoMinds (Mind 2007; Mind 2011) to the Natural Growth Project at the Medical Foundation for the Care of Victims of Torture (Linden and Grut 2002). The Natural Growth Project is a pioneering horticultural therapeutic project established at the Medical Foundation for the Care of Victims of Torture. At the project, psychotherapy takes place in garden allotments and also in a Remembrance Garden, where people are able to remember those that they have lost, remnants of their previous lives and come to terms with the trauma that they have experienced. This project is an example of nature being used both as a medium of communication and as a source of healing itself. People that have been involved in the project talk of profound, life-changing healing taking place (Linden and Grut 2002). The value of working with nature as a source of healing is described as 'nature as sanctuary, as balm to soothe our troubled souls' (Linden and Grut 2002, p. 18). As one of the clients of the project articulated 'When I garden I feel I have a painkiller medicine to make me strong' (Linden and Grut 2002, p. 44). Another client described the healing experience thus: 'It is the space and time I'm giving to myself on the land that has allowed me to clean my heart ... I believe that the work is holy' (Linden and Grut 2002, p. 30). This re-connection is particularly important and central to therapeutic work with people that have often been incarcerated and denied access to fresh air and natural light. While most of us and those people that we work with might not have had such harrowing experience, we are all able to benefit from taking time out to nurture and sustain our natural environment, and in doing so nurture and sustain ourselves (see Exercise 6.3).

Exercise 6.3 Garden, grow, nurture and sustain

This exercise can form part of a longer-term therapeutic project. Encourage your client (and/or yourself) to think about a creative way to renovate, revive or grow a patch of earth, window box or plant pot. Tend to the earth, feed it, feel it, and give new life to it. Planting something edible enforces further the connection with the earth.

Encourage your client to reflect on the experience.

What is different about the experience compared to their usual mode of experiencing?

What lessons is the earth urging your client to face?

The physical connection with the earth, with soil and rejuvenation can be healing in itself, and the metaphors that the natural world shows us, about seasonality, care, pace, time and compassion can have profound impacts too.

Nature and grief

The metaphors that we considered in the gardening Exercise 6.3 also point us towards the boundaries of life and death. In nature, we are born, grow and flourish, continually aging and moving towards the end of our life, at least as we know it. The natural world can teach us a great deal about this process and help us come to terms with the finality of our existence, and time in nature can be healing for people in the midst of the pain of grief. Harper's beautiful and emotional account of being in wilderness while he was grieving describes his experience of being with nature's rhythm: 'We followed exactly what was before us, and as the day wore on I found myself softening to and accepting whatever emerged inside' (Harper 1995, p. 184). In being more in tune with his natural rhythms his emotional experience flowed without check and he was sustained by the nature around him: 'My heart and belly felt expansive, and gradually I was overcome by the strangest sensation of webs connecting me with all that was around' (Harper 1995, p. 184). There was a sense of complete absorption and immersion in the experience, akin to the sort of 'flow' experiences suggested by Csikszentmihalyi as likely to bring about a sense of happiness and wellbeing (Csikszentmihalyi 1990).

In the interviews that I undertook focusing on transformation in nature, it was significant that the majority of participants placed their transformative experiences in the context of difficult periods of life (Macgregor 2013). Notably, grief and loss ran like a thread throughout many of the narratives. During very painful times, people described how it had been difficult to be present just in the moment, and how being in nature seemed to help facilitate this. Something about being in nature helps facilitate acceptance of pain and loss as part of the cycle of life. People also describe feeling more present and aware of their holistic experience immersed in nature, and feeling present helps shift perspective and resilience when people are in the midst of overwhelming pain. Part of this sense of being present might relate to connecting with what is *not* known or completely understood in the natural world, and yet having a trusting faith in existence.

Experiencing profoundly beautiful nature helps transcend pain and distress, shining a light on a different part of experience, feeling awe inspiring and calming at the same time.

Implications for practice

1. Being in nature can facilitate emotional healing. Encourage your clients and yourself to take part in an audit of the relationship between self and nature. Creatively consider ways to spend more time in nature and broaden awareness and focus on the natural world.

2. Consider how to build nature-based rituals into daily living. Use these as a particular reminder of connection and of how we are part of nature, rather than being distinctly separate entities.

3. In painful emotional times often people coming to therapy are trying to make sense of experience through words and cognitive understanding. Using nature's metaphors, of life-cycles, seasons and weather can help put words and images to difficult, hard-to-grasp life experiences.

4. Nature reminds us that there is much that we cannot fully grasp yet we are able to accept. Taking a problem, or a painful experience into nature, perhaps through walking meditation, can be very emotionally healing and helpful, particularly when we feel stuck.

5. Trusting in the healing potential of being in nature might require a leap of faith. This is understandable, given how far removed we are from nature's rhythms in everyday life. Aim to focus at a very basic level on being outside. Taking in deep breaths, expanding our horizons and focusing on a wider landscape can facilitate greater wellbeing.

6. Sometimes immersion experiences in nature can facilitate understanding and awareness at a deep level that is painful, in the same way as other psychotherapy practices can. It is important to be aware and informed.

7. Ensure that if you are taking excursions into nature you stay safe and be risk aware.

7

Who am I?

[P]sychology took for granted an intentional subject: the biographical 'me' that was the agent and the sufferer of all 'doings'. For most of its history, psychology located this 'me' within human persons defined by their physical skin and their immediate behaviour.

(Hillman 1995, p. xxvii)

One of the central tasks that people bring to the therapy room is the rather overwhelming question 'Who am I?'. Any enquiry or discussion that attempts to tackle the question 'Who am I?' inevitably has at its heart the idea of some sort of 'self'. Often therapy is perceived to be a journey of getting to know what 'I' want or perhaps how to balance 'self' needs with the need of 'those other people out there'. Understanding the 'self' has become an important modern pursuit, as self-help bookshelves will testify. When I was writing the draft this chapter one of my daughters, Lily, noticed the chapter title on a paper copy. 'Who am I', she said, 'That should be the chapter right at the beginning'. This got me thinking once again about the extent to which, in our selfie-ridden age, we have embraced the idea of the self being the central focus of life so that it becomes an automatic, engrained way of thinking about life so that any other focus is considered rather alternative.

Facing limitations of language

Language creates something of a problem right at the starting point of any critical discussion about the Western separation of self, other and nature. While acknowledging the complexities and limitations of language here, we will nevertheless endeavour to question these distinctions between self, other and world. In this chapter we will examine how understanding our self as part of a natural holistic system has the potential to reframe how we feel about ourselves, and particularly feelings of isolation and solitude. Using the four dimensions as a framework shows how placing our being in the natural world at the centre of each of the dimensions of our existence shifts the sense of self and connection. Critical evaluation of the notion of personality will facilitate discussions about the problems inherent in 'fixing' ourselves. Questions raised will focus on 'Who am I when I am in nature?'; 'How does nature help uncover connection with self experience?'; 'What matters when I am in my experience, aside from social rules and norms?'. Exercises will include nature-focused practices that can help us and our clients move towards greater insights and self-awareness.

The self: in or out of context?

The way that we conceptualize self as a standalone static entity is mirrored, as we discussed in earlier chapters, in our approach to mental health and to how we practise therapy. More often than not clients or patients are approached as isolated entities, their personalities hardly inter-dependent on their physical, social or spiritual context. Much of mainstream psychotherapy and mental health practice assumes that the boundary of self is something of a given. Coming from a different perspective, eco-psychologists place the question of the boundary of self at the core of their writing. Hillman (1995) asks searching questions about what he thinks of as the central issue at the crux of all psychology. *'Where is the "me"*? Where does the "me" begin? Where does the "me" stop. Where does the "other" begin?' (Hillman 1995, p. xxvii).

The practice of psychotherapy does not happen in a void, and the demands, aspirations and frames of reference of our age are mirrored both in the content of what people bring into therapy and the attitude with which they approach the dilemmas of everyday life. There is an assumption that the aim of psychotherapy and counselling to change an aspect of self or sometimes that of another person. This stands in contrast to an existential approach, where the aim of psychotherapy and counselling is to clarify and make sense of life through a process of exploration focused on bringing to light what makes life meaningful (Deurzen 2012). This is only possible if 'the client is willing and ready to examine the crucial issues and to question her basic assumptions' (Deurzen 2012, p. 16). This entails understanding and addressing assumptions about what is meant by self and personality, relationship and connection. One of Heidegger's important challenges to us was to stop letting ourselves be consumed by the world of objects and other people (Heidegger 1962). Heidegger urged a focus on dynamic existence lived in time which stands in contrast to ideas around fixed, rigid ideas of self (Heidegger 1962).

Boundaries of self

The words that we use to talk about our existence do not help in encouraging enquiry into our relational experience, since they construct polarities: self and other; you and me; I and thou; man and beast; client and therapist; inner and outer are just some examples. There is little room for focus on the important in-between-ness, for reflecting on fluid boundaries and soft, permeable, relational edges. Person-centred approaches tend to view the self in less of an interconnected, relational way than in existential philosophy, though the father of person-centred therapy, Carl Rogers, did write about the importance of valuing our particular place as part of a larger universal structure (Rogers 1951). Rogers spoke of each individual person being at the centre of their own world, though he acknowledged that what we saw as the human tendency to move towards growth is a formative tendency that is part of the make-up of our universe (Rogers 1978). Rogers also suggested that we cultivate a deep sense of our place in the universe in order to understand ourselves, acknowledging the importance of focusing on wider existence (Rogers 1978).

Existential philosophers have spent a great deal of time and effort on grappling with the relational aspect of life. Heidegger's Dasein, translated into 'being-in-the-world', actively opposes the isolation of a person from relationship, the removing of a person from the world (Heidegger 1962). Heidegger's writing acknowledges the interconnected basis of living and being (Heidegger 1962). In a similar vein, in his famous writings on existentialism and humanism, Sartre asks us to consider what we understand, as existentialists, when we say that '"existence precedes essence"? We mean that man first of all exists, encounters himself, surges up in the world – and defines himself afterwards' (Sartre 1946, p. 29). From Sartre's perspective, the self or 'I' that we define (for us or for other people) arises out of our firm existence in the world, out of our relational context, rather than us being a predefined, firmly boundaried personality entity implanted onto an already present world (Sartre 1946). Heidegger's writing proposes that the 'compound expression of "Being-in-the-World" indicates in the very way we have coined it, that it stands for a unitary phenomenon. This primary datum must be seen as a whole' (Heidegger 1962, p. 78). Heidegger's description of the relationship between natural world and human existence tries to dispel the conception of distinct unique entities, placing 'world' as integral to any awareness of being (Heidegger 1962, p. 78). Heidegger's views on being in time challenge the idea of fixedness by suggesting that we are never stationary. We are always moving in relationship and in time, passing from our past towards a future, making grasping a fixed, permanent sense of who we are a fruitless task (Heidegger 1962, p. 78). Deurzen describes Heidegger's challenge to us beautifully: 'we can allow ourselves to stand out in our appraisal of our past reality, our present situation and our future possibility, in what Heidegger terms the ec-stacy (standing out), which is a form of self and life-awareness' (Deurzen 2012, p. 6). The concept of life-awareness shifts the boundary through which we view existence and the frame of reference and horizon from which we approach wellbeing.

Heidegger's writing also shares something of the ethos of the eco-psychologists by suggesting that what matters is that we understand that any distinction that we make between self and others or self and world is subjective. Any distinction between self and nature is not a distinction marking two separate systems. So, we might make the mark at any point beginning with the boundary of our own body or, in Hillman's words 'we can take it as far out as we like – to the deep oceans and distant stars' (Hillman 1995, p. xix). We can also, as Roszak suggests, appreciate that we have choices around recognizing the uncertainty of making the cut, or marking the boundary, at all (Roszak et al. 1995).

Why does the boundary matter?

To begin with, let us think about where we routinely draw the boundary of self. Maiteny, an eco-therapist, notes that although we cannot *not* be part of the whole, we 'use the evolutionary gifts of our mind, consciousness, free will, intellect, imaginations, to insist on behaving as if we are not' (Maiteny 2012, p. 57). While Maiteny's writing is in the context of considering approaches to what he considers the environmental crisis of our times, his writing could equally be describing the mainstream approach to health, wellbeing and psychotherapy. When we begin to consider the boundary as being permeable we can open ourselves to the impact that being in the natural world can have on our emotional wellbeing and sense of self.

Self-experience in nature

Being in nature has the potential to increase and expand our experience of self in many different ways. Martin Milton described time that he spent in Africa and how these very special experiences give 'an opportunity for all our senses to makes themselves known and for us to respond fully to the world that we are a part of' in contrast to what he sees as more directed perception of life in urban environments (Milton 2008, pp. 39–40). During the research that I conducted on transformative experiences in nature, several key themes emerged relating to shifts in the experience of self (Macgregor 2013). I will expand on these, alongside the experiences of other writers, throughout this chapter.

Shifting self-awareness

Milton talks of self-awareness in remote nature. He describes this as 'qualitatively different from that experienced in the hustle and bustle of the concrete jungle', as the separation of 'experience and experiencer is exposed as being a very fragile construct' (Milton 2008, pp. 39–40). Harper's experience of wilderness practice shows that one of the most immediate experiences upon being in wild nature is sensory awareness and expansion, and that this awakening is a 'subtly powerful and underrated experience' (Harper 1995, p. 188). We experience a physical connection and alertness with, in and through nature. Being in nature intensifies experiences and our awareness; it brings 'many encounters which cannot be engineered or planned' (Brazier 2011, p. 31). What we reject or accept, embrace or distance in nature and wilderness also shows us something of what we embrace or not in ourselves. Nature holds a reflective mirror to our own values, judgements and anxieties.

A recurring theme in descriptions of being in nature is people's experience that their sense of self expands (Brazier 2011; Harper 1995; Milton 2008; Roszak et al. 1995). Greenway, an eco-psychologist, questioned 1,380 people that have passed through wilderness programmes. He noted how people tend to feel a sense of expansion and of re-connection with something important, feeling released from the repression of cultural norms and day-to-day practices (Greenway 1995).

Fixed limitations

Previous fixed limitations of self and identity seem to loosen when people are out in nature, particularly if they become immersed in natural processes, and people are surprised and sometimes feel quite overwhelmed by experiencing strengths and inner reserves that they were not previously aware of. These experiences often happen when people are outside of what they might usually find comfortable, facing an experience where they are anxious or afraid. As Camus wrote: 'In the depths of winter I at last discovered that there was in me an invincible summer' (Camus 1968, p. 169). Foster and Little (1987) describe the expansion of self and experience through extended wilderness trips as part of Vision Quests. Roads (1985) describes his powerful, transformative dialogue in nature: 'I was on this journey only because, after years of resistance, I was finally allowing a powerful inner reality to emerge' (Roads 1985, p. 42). As Roads 'clambered over an outcrop of smooth yet convoluted granite overlooking the gully' and the 'fresh foliage of the treetops swayed and danced ... An energy, wide open, expansive, and of light-filled proportion, swept around and through me' (Roads 1985, p. 42).

Dorothy's expanding sense of self

Dorothy grew up in England and lived in the city, until she married an American man and moved to the USA. She travelled from the East Coast to the West Coast of the USA by car, taking about two weeks to complete the journey. This was an extremely powerful experience that became an integral part of who she is. It was during this time that Dorothy experienced a profound transformation in nature. She was in her mid to late twenties at the time of this experience. She is now in her sixties and this experience has stayed with her over this time. The experience changed her attitude to being inside, and she now experiences anxiety if she knows that she is going to be inside for extended periods of time. The period of camping outside was a pivot point in Dorothy's life. She described how there was life before and life after that time. Decades later, Dorothy still seems slightly overcome by how important her first camping trip was, and how her life might have been if she hadn't had this experience.

It took Dorothy and her husband two weeks to travel from the East Coast to the West Coast of the USA. They decided that they would camp instead of staying each night in a motel. Dorothy described the newness of this experience, having never seen vistas like that before in England, and how she was completely awestruck. At the same time as being awestruck she also felt afraid, particularly of being outside in a tent in bear territory. She lived outside for the majority of the two weeks, and by the time she reached her destination in San Francisco, she had what she described as an epiphany: 'I don't want to live in a building! ... I don't want to; I didn't want to then go back to living in buildings. I'd realized something profound had happened to me in these two weeks of living in a tent and having more access to the natural world.' This was new territory for her, both literally and metaphorically, opening her to a raw feeling of experience and a vibrant sense of being really alive.

Dorothy felt that the experience of camping out during these two weeks was almost childlike, akin to the experience of Alice in Wonderland. It felt unreal, hard to believe that she was actually there, experiencing it, almost as if Dorothy was observing herself. Dorothy felt that a door was opened and she was able to see an experience for the first time. Without this experience, she feels that she would not be the person that she is today. When Dorothy saw what she described as an ocean of wheat fields she felt that it was at once both desolate and exquisite – that she had never seen such desolation before. She felt both awestruck and calmed by the experience.

On a separate occasion Dorothy went backpacking in a remote part of California. This was the first experience she had had of remote wilderness. She described how after a couple of days of moving into the wilderness there was nothing but her, her partner and nature. This experience shared some similarities with the experience she had of camping because there was some fear, particularly of bears. Dorothy felt it took her a couple of days to settle until all of the rhythms of the city had subsided. The period of settling felt like a process of exhaling and releasing. Dorothy lives in an urban environment now in a different country, and when she goes to the park she feels that her body relaxes in a similar way to having a long bath – she described the experience as her nature bath. If Dorothy is feeling 'a bit cranky' she goes out into the garden and feels much better, and the same with the park. These experiences are beneficial and help her feel better, both physically and emotionally.

Dorothy felt that being in nature was integral to her realization that love is not something 'out there' but something inside of her. Dorothy experienced a part of herself that she had not known before: she described this as the 'wild woman', not in terms of being crazy, but in terms of not being civilized and of being outside of social norms. This was the first time she had had this experience of what she talked of as a 'male' part of herself. It was very liberating and expanding.

Now when Dorothy talks about herself she feels happy and comfortable thinking about herself as the mountain girl, this wild woman. She feels happier with the rugged, wild lifestyle and experience that she first encountered on her journey in the USA. Her face lights up when she talks of this; she appears vibrant, alive and energized.

Dorothy feels that water is like her unchartered territory; that there is more for her to discover about herself in relationship to water than any other part of being in nature. Dorothy feels a particular kind of opening feeling when she is at expansive water (the sea or large lakes) that is different from other large vistas. Water is a little scarier for her than other parts of nature; there is more of a sense of the unknown. She compared this to the vastness of the night sky and how she feels insignificant in comparison to such scale. Dorothy feels that the water is somewhat like her unconscious or psyche. Considering the unseen depths is frightening and takes her outside of her everyday understanding of self.

Fixedness: A long-playing record

Let us think for a moment of how we fix or sediment ourselves as we try and hold on to an idea of who we are (Exercise 7.1). Existential therapists might hold that this attempt to 'fix' or capture ourselves as something of an essence is in part a reflection of our need to try and avoid the temporary nature of existence: to fix ourselves in the face of our death and non-being. Deurzen and Adams (2016) say that 'of all the dilemmas and tensions that we have to contend with, the tension between life and death is the most fundamental. None of us can avoid the remarkable irony that we are born to die. Ultimately everything is temporary' (Deurzen and Adams 2016, p. 121). Perhaps our attempt to try and grasp onto an idea of who we are is a way, in part, of rebutting the inevitability of our demise.

Exercise 7.1 Self-description and definition

This can be completed in pairs, or individually.

Spend a few minutes considering what you *think* about yourself and how other people might define you. Use the table below as inspiration and note words that you are either attracted to or drawn to reject. Please aim to write as detailed a description as possible.

Characteristics

Cold	warm	happy	sad	organized	bossy
dynamic	kind	motherly	fatherly	child-like	impulsive
leader	follower	team-player	loner	aggressive	pessimistic
optimistic	thoughtful	sensitive	over-achiever	perfectionist	
excitable	impetuous	creative	methodical	bullying	
resentful	aggravating	annoying	resilient	energetic	
soulful	spiritual	egotistical	narcissistic	middle child	
eldest	baby	angry	loving	demonstrative	
healing	plodder	brag	advocate	charitable	sexual
sensual	tactile				

_____

_____

_____

_____

_____

_____

_____

_____

_____   ▶

◄

Once you have written your description, consider how you experience yourself at this moment, right now. If you are completing this exercise in pairs or larger groups, each person can help the other to explore their present experience. Begin to reflect on the words that you have written about yourself. Consider how your description of yourself relates to how you are feeling now. Are there words that, in your present experience, do not hold true for you?

Spending time in nature helps facilitate a more present awareness of ourselves and our world, enabling us to shake the narrow or more rigid self-concepts that we often hold on to. If we use the clouds in the sky as a metaphor for example, it is impossible for us to grasp a definition of a cloud in the sky; as we observe it or try and define it, it evolves in structure and form. The natural world inspires and invites us to face our existence as it is now in time, without having to grab onto a strong definition and with an open mind about where the boundaries reside and to what extent we want to uphold them.

Awareness of self in relationship

The experience of self as *part of* something bigger, as connected with environment, increases in nature in contrast to the feeling of a self that is limited by the boundaries of a physical body.

Personal life experiences are approached less analytically as a result of being in nature (Macgregor 2013). There is a shift in awareness that relates to an experience of feeling a *more authentic knowledge*; what is described as a *sensory wisdom*. Part of this is as a result of holding social structures and rules more lightly in nature and feeling more centred in life experience. Sometimes there is a feeling of nature helping uncover feelings and experiences that have been smothered by social rules or by other people. It is as if the day-to-day rules are up for discussion when we take ourselves out of our usual social environment and immerse ourselves in the present of the natural world.

Being in nature helps confront our present being in a way that can feel raw and painful as well as cathartic and therapeutic. If nature facilitates us being more in touch with a more authentic knowledge, then this will inevitably include the difficult, distressing parts of life that perhaps we routinely try to avoid. During research interviews one of the themes that I was not anticipating was the degree of emotional pain that was described in nature: that stripping ourselves of the usual social rules can be as raw as it is liberating. Grief ran as a theme throughout: being in nature seemed to facilitate people being able to face and accept a level of pain that was greater than in more day-to-day life without feeling overwhelmed or rushing to fix it, change it or deny it.

In my own experience, when I was grieving in the mountains I felt more in touch with an essential quality of my emotional experience that I felt unable to find and express when I was not in such awe-inspiring nature (see personal case example later in this chapter). This was related in part to a lack of social constraints; to being able to accept my emotional experience as part of the present moment of being. It also related to the feeling of increased bodily awareness and a felt sense and understanding of experience, moving away from a more cognitive or rational bias. Part of the increase in self-acceptance and decrease in self-consciousness in nature is also in being very absorbed in enjoying the physical, sensory side of being in nature. Outside of the moment, on reflection, there is a sense of a little of the self-consciousness returning, albeit with the understanding that the experience is important and valued.

Knowing self-experience

There is a feeling of knowing oneself in the midst of feeling connected and part of nature, a profound and crucial connection with self-experience. Being in nature is often described as feeling like returning to a home point, or base point of *life, as if being in touch with experiencing.*

Exercise 7.2 helps us to focus on broadening our awareness to think about our part of the whole.

**Exercise 7.2 Focusing on broadening awareness of who
_we_ are**

For the purposes of this exercise you will need to suspend the more usual view
of who you are and adopt something of the attitude of connectedness of the
eco-psychologists.

Go outside and focus on a plant in nature, a leaf on a tree or a flower on a bush.
(If at all possible please do try and undertake this exercise outside in nature. If
this is not possible, focus on an image online or in a book that situates a flower
or leaf in its natural habitat.)

Now describe the flower or leaf in as much detail as possible. What is the shape
of it? How does it relate to its surroundings? How is the temperature, wind, sunlight or rain shaping or changing it?

Now consider your relationship to it. Touch it, hold it, feel its texture, inhale its
scent. How do you relate to it? What is the sensory experience of touching it
like for your skin? Consider how you fit into the nature that you are; in the same
way that the soil is connected to the plant, the earth sustains you and the sunlight and air that touches your skin is the same sunlight and air that nourishes
the plant and makes it thrive.

Breathe slowly and deeply. Try and be present in the experience and appreciate
the web of threads that forms the interconnection that your existence is part of.

Either 'out there' or 'in here'

As discussed at the beginning of this chapter, the question that we ask
in therapy is often based around 'Who am I?'. We assume bodily boundaries around this question. Exercise 7.2 allowed us to move towards
thinking about what we usually talk of as 'out there' as more a part of
who we are. There is a significant difference between the questions that
we ask for ourselves (the 'inner' side of the boundary) and those that
we ask of 'out there'. If we return to the object that we focused on in
Exercise 7.2 and consider our attitude to it compared to our attitude to
ourselves we will find some differences. For example, when I appreciate
something in nature I tend not to wish that it is qualitatively different
to how I find it (perhaps with the exception of weather) whereas many
of the clients that I work with spend a great deal of time and effort

trying to mould or shape themselves into a different version. An important difference is that we tend to appreciate nature with a great deal more fluidity than we do other people or ourselves. We allow the tree and other vegetation to evolve its structure, its quality, shed its leaves and regrow with an attitude of acceptance that is very different from the way in which we tend to fix ourselves into straightjackets of personalities. And even where we do impose a degree of fixedness on other species or on parts of the natural world it is with an acceptance far removed from how we would approach our own characters or 'traits'.

Transformation of self-perception

Changes in experience of self are often gradual and unfolding in relation to being in nature. Transformation in self-perception can be particularly powerful and is also linked to more holistic awareness: a sense of playfulness that is discovered and wondered about, a feeling of being more than just an intellect; for example, having experiences that fall outside of a previous self-construct. Being in nature seems to draw the person into a very present focus, and this itself is central to the transformation of self-perception since it shifts the focus towards experience and away from definitions of self. At the same time, social conventions and rules also recede into the background, enabling present self-experience to be more easily accepted.

For people that have had powerful experiences in nature, there is an urge to nurture the nature–self relationship, and more widely to be more engaged with environmental issues, and to return to nature to replicate transformative experiences. As well as looking to nature for experiences that feel particularly transformative, there is a desire to keep in contact with nature on a day-to-day basis in order to increase daily wellbeing. Developing these sorts of routines can have a significant impact on wellbeing.

Emotional experience

Feelings, thoughts and embodied awareness are sometimes more directly accessed in nature without us feeling that they are thwarted by social rules relating to ideas of what is appropriate or what should or should not be accessible or expressed. This can feel liberating, though it involves the gamut of emotional experience meaning that grief, pain, loss, anger and the like are also more directly felt and confronted, as we discussed earlier. Personal life experiences are sometimes approached less analytically and there is a shift in awareness related to feeling what is sometimes described as a more authentic knowledge. This is akin to Brazier's description of nature as it 'unsettles our habitual ways of interacting with life' (Brazier 2011, p. 35). Knowledge, particularly in terms of what matters to us and what we feel, seems to arise more spontaneously when we are present in nature.

The interaction between the social and personal dimensions

Towards an inner locus of evaluation

In my research, part of the transformative aspect of being in nature was expressed as feeling freer from the 'shoulds' and 'oughts' that are experienced in society: as a liberation from everyday rules and constraints so that present experiences are more easily accessed as they are, rather than under or within a layer of social meaning. In such experiences, there is a movement towards valuing experience without an idea of whether it is socially appropriate. Indeed, this leads to some degree of self-consciousness talking about the experience within social settings as it is sometimes difficult to reflect on outside of the moment because speaking within usual social settings, sitting inside, already changes something of the experience. There is an understanding and experiential appreciation of the arbitrary nature of many social constructs and getting away from everyday life is a key part of many of the transformative experiences. Getting away from social stresses is an important part: while this is often geographical, sometimes it is more symbolic or metaphorical, in that some experiences were described in such language even though they took place in the same environment as everyday social life.

Social aspect of self

Profound experiences in nature change the experience of the person in their relationships with other people. Part of this is feeling more accepting of the present and of self. There is a realization that one does not have to pretend to be something – a feeling akin to deeply relaxing, exhaling, letting go. There is sometimes a different quality to personal relationships in nature: more creative and open encounters. Both the quality and content of the dialogue are embedded in the physical context. As physical boundaries become more organic and natural, so social relationships seem to open out and expand. One of the research participants described walking across a hillside with someone else and falling into a different sort of rhythm than they would have done if they were inside, which seemed to facilitate the dialogue and relationship becoming more creative as they walked alongside each other.

Present experience and personal meaning

Although the return from nature involves a renewed acquaintance with social structures, the experience of having been immersed in nature impacts on understanding and perception that is taken into ongoing meanings, values and intentions. Brazier describes coming 'face to face with the deep truth of existence' in nature (Brazier 2011, p. 34). It is as if nothing seems to smother the present, almost a feeling of helplessness at having to accept what is: being within an experience as it arises. This feeling of being very *present in relation* shifts thoughts and worries about the future and past, and is therefore noted as particularly powerful by people who had had ongoing traumatic or difficult life experiences (Macgregor 2013). Part of this feeling of losing or letting go of control of what is outside of the present moment is liberating and is a release and relief, resonating with Heidegger's description of gelassenheit or releasement (Heidegger 1962).

Spending time in nature can facilitate a clarity of experience and a focus on what actually matters, linking personal emotional experience and more spiritual values, leading to the sort of 'dramatic breakthroughs' highlighted by Kanner and Gomes (1995, p. 91). This has a pre-reflective quality to it so that the experiencing seems to point towards and drive the construction of meaning, rather than meaning being applied to experience after the fact. Being with experience that feels more free from social rules and constraints seems to allow space for personal meaning to evolve out of the experience, resonating with Greenway's account of how people re-connect with something important when they feel liberated from social norms (Greenway 1995).

The transformation of self and nature

An awareness seems to arise in transformative experience in nature of the self being part of a larger whole, rather than self and nature as separate entities. Heidegger's (1962) assertion that 'Being-in-the-world shall first be made visible with regard to that item of its structure which is the "world" itself' (Heidegger 1962, p. 91) is supported by the transformative experiences in nature where this felt knowledge of being part of a whole arises *in* awareness, rather than as meaning applied *after* the experience. Research participants described resonating with the question, 'who am I?' in nature and feeling less certain about usual self/other constructs and boundaries. The sense of being part of nature is liberating, since it seems to highlight the limits to power and choice that we have in the context of the greater system. There is a sense of belonging in nature that helps diminish isolation, particularly where the individual feels isolated from other people emotionally, or where particular experiences and feelings are not understood or accepted as appropriate in the social world. To some extent nature is referred to, and experienced as, a significant, often idolized other – an active participant in a relationship rather than the more objectified focus of place that is perhaps more familiar to us.

Transformative experiences involve a feeling of freeing more fixed ideas of self-definition, getting to understand and accept self on a wider, more holistic level, and sometimes losing a sense of self when the boundaries and fixed ideas of self dissolve more radically. This seems to resonate with Sartre's writings about existence preceding essence, as if the present moment of experience in nature is the experience of surging up in the world that Sartre talks of prior to it being constructed and defined into a something, into an essence (Sartre 1946, p. 29). The paradox of both feeling a greater sense of self and losing self relates to the difference between self as structure and self as experience, again correlating with Sartre's writings (Sartre 1946, p. 29). There is a greater awareness and understanding of appreciation of self-experience in relation to existence and a loss of isolated sense of self as the sense of connection with and being part of nature increases. This relates back to the earlier discussion on movement towards valuing experience with fewer social constructs, and leads to an increase in knowing one's experience and to experiencing parts of self that are sometimes valued less in a particular social environment. For example, one of my research participants felt that she valued particular physical qualities in nature whereas in her usual social and work environment such qualities were deemed unimportant and as a result she felt she usually distanced this part of her life experience (Macgregor 2013).

The loss of self that is described arises from the strength of connection with nature that is experienced in the powerful moment. This resonates with Hillman's writings about the location of the threshold of self and other, and his assertion that these are arbitrary delineations (Hillman 1995). This feels deeply spiritual, linking experience across all of the dimensions (see Chapter 8 for further discussion). Hillman describes how we cannot be sure where to demarcate self and other, and indeed that self might not all be internal; indeed, it might be 'out there' (Hillman 1995, p. xix). The idea, then, of connecting with something is to some extent thrown in the air, since the notions of inner and outer, self and other are required to support such an idea. This is also in line with a systemic approach to self and relationship, as outlined by Bateson (1972), and his critique of constructions of world as inanimate object separated from self. Part of the loss of self is an increased appreciation of the self as being environmentally dependent, existing in relationship rather than as an isolate. Understanding self in a more relational frame leads to an increase in the potential for different experiences as ideas of what an individual can or cannot do, is or is not as a person, take on less certainty and significance. This increases optimism and feelings of expanded potential towards the future as more possibilities are opened.

Personal case example

My doctoral research was a heuristic journey into transformative experiences in nature that was born from my growing awareness of the importance of nature in my life. I count myself exceptionally lucky to have spent my childhood and most of my adult life living in beautiful countryside with very easy access to woodlands, rivers, hilltops and open countryside. Many of my childhood summer holidays were spent in Snowdonia and each time I drove towards the mountains on my way to the wet, windy beaches of the North Wales coastline I felt a strong, exciting feeling of coming home. During my adult life I stayed away from mountains for some years, until I first went skiing. I am notorious among my family and friends for being possibly the worst skier to ever have flung themselves down the side of an alpine slope, and being rather competitive it took more than a few attempts (and rather a lot of money and some rather blue language) at the beginner's class for me to admit that I would never be able to ski as well as the toddlers whizzing past me down the mountainside. Yet, what skiing did give me was a re-connection with awe-inspiring nature and (after I had quit trying to prove something) extended periods of time to immerse myself in the mountains away from the ski factories in the sky. Part of the catalyst for choosing to focus on transformative experiences in nature was the death of my grandmother on New Year's Eve while I was not skiing on a ski holiday in Switzerland. After I had heard the very sad news from my father that my grandmother had died, and after I had bundled children off to their various lessons I set out on my own into crisp snow at 3,000 metres and began to walk away from the resort into the unknown virgin snow. The experience was profound for me, and was one of the moments that I chose to focus on as I explored the phenomenon of my research study.

The death of my grandmother and my grief in Saas Fe

Being in nature felt vital to my experience of grief and I felt urgently drawn out into the wilderness of the mountain range, out into the snow where I was staying. Nature helped me express and experience my pain and loss more fully and openly than I thought possible, and certainly than I had thought possible from previous experiences of similar loss. Even in intense grief, being in nature helped me feel calmer and more peaceful, as if I was more in touch with a deeper holistic experience and able to accept how I felt without layers of 'shoulds' and 'oughts' smothering my experience. The physical experience of being nature was critical to the expansion of my embodied emotional awareness and restoring a mind/body equilibrium.

When I was in the mountains I experienced my grief as a catalyst for a renewed and sustained urgency to live more vitally and this experience was the foundation for major changes in my life over the following couple of years, including being the precursor to focusing on nature in my studies and this writing. I had a strong sense of understanding and accepting very painful feelings because of the connection I felt in the beauty of nature. I was only aware of this experience on reflection; it felt effortless at the time, a very real sense of being in the right place for me. My feelings seemed more fluid in nature, and I have felt this at other times since, particularly when facing personal difficulties and during challenging times.

At other times when I have been in nature, lying on the ground, on earth, rock, or grass, I have felt connected with something important, although I find this difficult to articulate and define and it leaves me feeling self-conscious and exposed. I am aware that I connect with, listen to and trust in my bodily feelings and experiences to a much greater extent in nature. My sometimes rigid, segmented self-critical voices are integrated and transformed into a greater level of embracing and enveloping self-acceptance and self-care.

Outside of my experience of grief in nature, on other occasions there is a dancing, energetic quality to some of my experience of this relationship, a sense of lightness and liberation. My felt sense of my emotions is deeper and lower in my body, relating again to a loss of judgemental self-talking based on social norms and self-expectations that allows me to be more in touch with my embodied experience. I value being in touch with my bodily rhythms when I am out walking, as opposed to the more normal social time structures, such as artificial mealtimes and bedtimes. This helped me feel a sense of being in harmony with my environment, a feeling of being at home. Emotionally, when I shut my eyes and sat still on rocks in the mountains I felt completely awakened to a broader, deeper and expansive aliveness, that felt like some sort of spiritual connection. This sense of looking outwards, towards and beyond the self remains a routine feeling of being in nature for me, at the same time as feeling solidly grounded in sensory and felt experience.

My relationship with nature feels trustful and dependable, reassuring and life-affirming as if I am increasing my awareness of some essential presence. Nature has provided me with an emotional and existential metaphor of turbulent storms being weathered inside and out. Yet it also awakens other vulnerabilities – affirming death and the transitory quality of each moment.

My time focus shifts in nature and I have experienced letting go of what was outside of the moment, a present focus that seemed to happen without any effort – in complete contrast with the effort I make to be more present in day-to-day life. I experienced a sense of stillness and being in time that felt special. Even in very difficult emotional feelings, I had a sense of wellbeing grounded in a feeling of 'this is what I am and what I have right now'. Standing on the edge of the cloud in the mountains I described feeling 'just right there, right in the, like right in the middle of some.... right at the heart of something and yet all of it at the same time'. This moment was beautiful and energetic; it felt satisfying and enough. There was no need for anything other at that moment. It remains difficult for me to articulate how privileged I feel that my precious relationship with nature is, because it feels fundamental to my sense of self and life when I am in nature. I am more aware of my *place in time in nature*; the ancient, timeless quality of natural landscapes links me to people that I have lost, as well as to those that will be born. There is a sense of isolation and belonging that I experience as being held in tension. Watching the mist blowing over the barren landscape showed something of the constant, transitory evolution and connected me with a sense of profound loss. The poignant sadness in each goodbye, and the pain of each eventual end seemed echoed in every minute change as time passed, as if it resonated in the constant evolution of the landscape. I also feel that being in nature seems to throw my normal notions of 'self' on their head, as I question the boundaries between self and environment. At the same time as feeling deeply connected to nature, expanding into it, I have a deep and crucial realization of an innate experience of self. I experience my relationship with the natural world as similar to a faith, since I trust in the experience yet without fully understanding. There is a sense of the ineffable.

When I return back from being in wild nature, particularly from being in mountains, to a daily routine, something from the experience remains, so that I feel more self-aware and in touch with my felt experience in everyday life. Notions of comfort are challenged and expanded in nature and, at a particularly important moment of transformation in nature, I experienced a shift in not wanting to remain safely in my comfort zone. As a result, being true to my experience of being in the world seems to take precedence over being comfortable. Nature seems to point to authenticity in opposition to much of what I have experienced in society.

Implications for practice

1. We need to challenge everyday ideas of what 'self' is if we are to open up the potential of more holistic experience. Holding lightly social understandings of self and personality is important in establishing more relational/connected psychotherapy practice.

2. Being out in nature helps us appreciate fluidity and being in constant change in contrast to fixedness. Fixed ideas of self limit us and the potential of our relationships. Paying attention to the contradictions in how we judge ourselves compared to our attitude to different facets of nature can help nudge us out of rigid understandings and attitudes.

3. The boundary between self and other; self and nature, can be considered as an arbitrary one. Existential psychotherapists and eco-practitioners would argue that any distinct separation we make is artificial and takes us away from the context that we are embedded in. Life is neither 'in here' or 'out there' but in the in-between.

4. Our sense of self and awareness feels expanded in nature. Spending time immersed in nature enables us to have fresh insights and renewed energy.

5. Being in nature can help us experience our emotions more authentically. This can mean that we access both painful and more happy emotions more fully.

8

A Spiritual Existence

Being in the depths of wild nature has the potential to touch people at a deeply profound, spiritual level. Religious and spiritual figures at the heart of a variety of faiths have sought solace and wisdom in the natural world. In this chapter we will focus on the potential for transformative experiences in the natural world and how these might provide opportunities for both re-connection and for the pursuit of enlightenment. We will draw on Maslow's (1970) description of peak experiences to look at the potential for these sorts of occurrences in nature. A detailed exploration of nature and the spiritual dimension will focus on the impact of peak experiences on mental health and wellbeing, and on the essential human need to connect holistically to nature and to feel part of the natural universe. So that we can relate these ideas to examples of current problems in living, we will consider psychological issues of both addiction and depression and evaluate them in the context of the human need for 'nature highs' and what happens when these experiences are thwarted or neglected. As human beings, we need experiences that take us out of the mundanity of day-to-day living. Questions raised will include 'What does an individual's part in the wider universe mean?' and 'What can be taken from peak experiences into everyday living for both clients and practitioners?'.

Nature and spirituality

Being in wild nature touches people at a deep spiritual level and these experiences are often described as peak or pivotal: religious figures at the centre of many faiths sought solace and salvation in nature, from Jesus in the desert to Buddha in the forest. Many descriptions of transformative experiences seem to have a spiritual impression about them – a sense of mystery, acceptance and faith in some natural system or order, and a sense of the occurrence being beyond words, such as those outlined by Foster and Little (1987) and in Jung's writings (1967). Later in this chapter we will consider how people feel a sense of interconnection and that they are part of something larger. This is akin to descriptions of Buddhist enlightenment – where a person comes to see life and the world with a clarity without the many overlays that are a result of experiencing the world from the perspective of a separate self, rather than through intrinsic interconnection. It is this sort of connected experience that people describe in relation to being in nature, along with a sense of expansive freedom. Heidegger (2010) uses the German term *gelassenheit*, translated to mean 'releasement', to describe letting go or letting be, and the original German word is related to a religious or existential letting-go and letting-be (Heidegger 2010, p. xi). Religions across time place nature and our connection to earth at their heart, perhaps most notably the pantheistic correlation that equates God or divinity with nature and the universe. Goodenough (1998), in her discussion of emergent religious principles, describes how we find ourselves on a planet that is perfect for our existence: 'We arrived, but a moment ago, and found it to be perfect for us in every way. And then we came to understand that it is perfect because we arose from it and are part of it' (Goodenough 1998, p. 168).

In his description of peak experiences, Maslow noted that the idea of 'sacred' can become split off or separated from the world of nature (Maslow 1970). Once it is split off it tends to be correlated with particular rituals and practices; particular ways of life. This splitting off does not make the discussion and exploration of spiritual experiences easy, since they sit outside of the world of the concrete and rational that are more readily explainable and which present Western society so obviously favours. Maslow wrote about the very beginning of high religion being the 'private, lonely, personal illumination' of some prophet or seer (Maslow 1970, p. 19). It is these sorts of transformative experiences that people describe in relation to being in nature.

Nature is sometimes considered as divine and becomes an almost personified focus of religion, akin to worshipping a deity, and indigenous cultures throughout time have worshipped nature (Macgregor 2013). There is a sense of feeling connected in nature that can sometimes feel part of a divine or more important order that is trusted and accepted, even when life does not make sense on a personal level. Morgan describes this in terms of experiencing enlightenment in nature; taking us outside of and beyond our usual self-experience (Morgan 1998). People experience a feeling of nature being an integral part of this experience, rather than 'place' being a backdrop or insignificant; the background in which experience occurs. This is a juxtaposition to the notion of separate experience and experiencer, something that Milton referred to as 'being a very fragile construct' (Milton 2008, pp. 39–40).

My research on transformative experiences in nature endeavoured to capture the detail of such experiences and what such a phenomenon is like across all of the dimensions of existence (Macgregor 2013).

Spirituality and peak experiences in nature: An overview

People that have had transformative experiences in nature have offered rich descriptions of experiencing a feeling of moving towards what is not understood or what has not been previously experienced, along with a sense of personal expansion. I will draw on these descriptions, which resonate with writings across the eco-therapy and eco-psychology fields, in this chapter (Macgregor 2013). There are parts of being in nature and having peak or transformative experiences that feel unreal or surreal, that are difficult to capture, that seem magical, ethereal and full of wonder, akin to the sorts of spiritual feelings that Foster and Little (1987) described and that are acknowledged as being somewhat difficult to put into words. Time might seem suspended in such moments, which are powerful peak points of the kind outlined by Maslow (1970) as being visions of heaven, transcending and transforming day-to-day life: captivating and enthralling us.

Nature is experienced as providing a connection with what is not seen and not experienced as well as what is seen and actually experienced. Experiences that are often unseen or mysterious, or difficult to articulate routinely tend to be conceived of under the 'spiritual' umbrella. However, in my research, experiences such as these seem strongly connected with the physical dimension: felt experiences that are difficult to verbalize. The physical and spiritual are intertwined. The sense of connection in nature that is also described as spiritual is located strongly in the physical dimension, being related in the physical universe that is vast and somewhat incomprehensible on both space and time dimensions. The incomprehensibleness of this vastness of place, history and future is inspiring, overwhelming and transformative and feels infinite – transcending routine personal understandings. Sometimes this can feel profoundly reassuring; it increases a sense of wonder and awe, at the same time as being a motivating and inspiring catalyst for living life dynamically and with urgency. People that have such powerful experiences reflect on how they shift meaning, alter perspective and ignite energy and motivation.

A life without peaks – a depressed experience

If we begin to consider life in our modern Western age in the context of Maslow's suggestion that peak or transformative experiences are potentially open to us all, we might begin to think about how we experience these sorts of 'natural highs', if so many of us are disconnected from the natural world for much of our day-to-day lives. We have seen in earlier chapters what might happen if we are cut off from nature's rhythms from a temporal perspective. What happens if we are disconnected from the potential of powerful, transformative experience? We might experience the sort of 'nature hunger' that Rust writes about (Rust 2008, p. 77) or we might feel the inner deadening that many people talk about when they describe feeling depressed. Disconnection from meaning, from a sense of purpose and from vibrancy, is often reported in people who are feeling dissatisfied and sad in and with their daily existence. At the same time, reaching out (either literally or metaphorically) to the outside world becomes increasingly difficult for people feeling depressed, and indeed such a diminished interest in life is one of the criteria for depressive disorders in the Diagnostic and Statistical Manual V (DSM V) (American Psychiatric Association (APA) 2013). Buzzell and Chalquist (2009) describe how people that have been taken on wilderness therapy experiences feel a sense of awe and wonder that they have previously lacked and a reawakening of a sense of belonging. For many people that have experienced these sorts of therapeutic benefits in nature, being in nature becomes a central enduring need in their lives for them to experience a sense of ongoing wellbeing (Buzzell and Chalquist 2009).

The search for highs and addiction

It does not take a great leap to begin to reflect on how a craving for peak experiences might underlie at least some of the problems in living that people report to psychotherapists. The experience of depression is often reported as a feeling of inner deadening, and anyone that has either experienced enduring depression or worked with clients in the midst of such experiences will appreciate the chasm between a depressed existence and peak experiences.

People struggling with all kinds of addictions frequently describe the 'high' that they feel and the need to revisit that high, to experience something that they do not feel routinely, that takes them outside of banality. The UK charity Action on Addiction UK describes addiction as an 'all-consuming relationship with a substance or behaviour that is driven by a conscious or unconscious desire to feel something different, which results in a range of harmful consequences' (Action on Addiction UK 2017). The notable point here is the 'desire to feel something different' (Action on Addiction 2017). That different feeling can cover a wide range of potential experiences, from not feeling anxious or worried or feeling relaxed to feeling euphoric. Sometimes there is a desire to lose oneself, to escape, to feel something outside of the difficult everyday. Peak experiences in nature are often described in remarkably similar terms, as we have seen in earlier chapters and the writings of the eco-psychologists. The *International Community for Eco-Psychology Journal* (2017) is just one home of many such descriptions where people describe activities from rock-climbing to sailing in terms more usually associated with religious or spiritual encounters; terms such as total zen, descriptions of losing oneself, feeling something greater and becoming totally at one with what is happening. These experiences resulting from being outdoors in nature are not all associated with taking part in adrenaline-related sporting activities. Such feelings are described by people taking part in wilderness journeys, spending time being still at the side of lakes and mountains, for example. Importantly, people have described having powerful, peak, transformative experiences at times when they were least expecting them and without any intention to seek such an encounter (Macgregor 2013).

Much of our day-to-day routine is rather disconnected from nature and being outside, and therefore from the peaks and troughs, highs and lows, of the natural world. In many ways this has provided us with a rather comfortable life. Who would want to live as our ancestors did, going to bed as dusk arrives, rising at dawn, eating only seasonal food, without the luxuries of heating, airtight shelter and technological conveniences that so many of us enjoy? We have already seen that the price that we pay for living a life slightly removed from our nature roots is a feeling of disconnection, of a slight but sometimes enduring deadening and under-appreciation of our physical dimension. Modern-day discourse usually equates spirituality with the mind and the soul; we do not explore our physicality in a quest for enlightenment or for making sense of life. The split that we have already addressed pushes these realms further apart, yet the yearnings for a 'high', an escape or awakening that are inherent in much of addiction often bridge and merge the physical and spiritual dimensions.

It is in the spiritual dimension where we move outside of our day-to-day mundanity, where our values rest, where we make and remake meaning and renew commitments to ourselves and other people. Deurzen outlines her understanding of the spiritual dimension, the Uberwelt (over-world), as a kind of meta-world where the rest of our more mundane day-to-day living is put into wider, more enduring context (Deurzen 2012). It is where we move beyond that which we make sense of and move towards the mysterious, the sacred and the extraordinary (Deurzen 2012). As well as the spiritual dimension being concerned with the meaning that we make of our existence, it concerns our personal values; what really touches us, those things that we ultimately live for and indeed might ultimately die for. This understanding of spirituality is not necessarily concerned with what we might understand as faith; nor does it assume an automatically ethereal or 'head'-based encounter, though neither is ruled out. In line with Maslow's writing, a more existential approach to spiritual experience can be a deeply physical, embodied moment of being.

Considering how we make time and space for peak, transformative experiences is important, as is realizing that they may lie outside of the more usual methods that people use to experience being 'out of their minds'.

Self-harm, deadening and re-awakening

According to the Mental Health Foundation, the UK has the highest rate of self-harming in Europe, with an estimated 400 out of every 100,000 people deliberately harming themselves, the majority between 11 and 25 years of age (Mental Health Foundation 2017). The actual figure is likely to be a great deal higher because of underreporting. Figures show that the rise in self-harm over the last 10 years has been dramatic, not least because of unprecedented social pressures. Other causes of the devastating increase include pressure to succeed, social media, body image, physical and sexual abuse and increasing sexualization of young people. One of the recurring themes that people who self-harm talk about is a need to feel alive or real – to fight a feeling of deadening, a numbness or disconnection (Alive 2017). There is no doubt that this is only one facet of what is often a very complex issue, yet it is something that fits with what we have discussed concerning the issue that the eco-psychologists see as a much wider deadening and disconnection. As we remove ourselves further from our biological environmental roots in nature we thwart our potential to feel truly alive. Given that our present world privileges the cognitive, technical and digital over the felt, sensory and wider holistic experience, our capacity for experiences that fall outside of the narrower, disembodied focus is routinely limited.

The meaning of transformative spiritual experiences

Experiences in nature provide a momentum and meaning to living related to the feeling of being part of a larger system. For people who talk of having transformative experience, the relationship with nature is often integral to their values, perspective and meaning of life. This is seen throughout the writings of eco-therapists: that there is a personal commitment to valuing the environment and the human–nature relationship; a reciprocity of sorts. Individuals' perspectives tend to shift to a more anthropocentric stance away from a human-centric attitude. Transformative experiences in nature urge people that have them to live more in line with their experiences, beliefs and values, and to embrace life and its opportunities. The experience translates across different facets of life, from work to relationships, and encourages a focus away from social rules as the locus of evaluation. Part of the impact on meaning is that people wish to step outside of what is comfortable and secure and reach towards experiences that matter and that feel expansive.

Silvester's spiritual awakening and healing

Several years ago, Silvester began to experience a significant shift in how he perceived what he described as 'this reality called Life'. Traversing a long period in his life that he referred to as 'the dark night of the soul', and suffering from extreme bouts of depression and hopelessness, he went into the forest over and over again and was able to glimpse a sigh of relief, which no other activity seemed able to provide. It was in those moments of communing with nature that he began to realize that nature would be his healer, strength, and his joy, offering substance and sustenance for him. As he reflected on the larger scale of suffering experienced by people throughout our society, Silvester began to feel strongly that the root issue is that human beings have become disconnected; dissociated from nature and the natural rhythms of life.

Silvester had a period of existential crisis that lasted many years. He had been employed in the corporate world and had felt uneasy with this, so had left to live in a yoga ashram. This did not bring him the comfort and peace that he was looking for, and he went further into an enduring existential crisis, searching for meaning and purpose in his life. He had many health problems, was feeling depressed and disconnected, and extremely tired. He moved back to the land of his birth and suffered major multiple bereavements of family members. This was a traumatic time. Trying to hold the remaining family together and to bear what was going on, Silvester also lost everything financially during this time. He had a sense of hopelessness, of isolation and utter despair that he felt never left him and he had recurring panic attacks. He would keep himself up at night and was totally exhausted to the point that he would just pass out.

During and after this traumatic time, while Silvester was trying to come to terms with his experience and feeling full of despair, he began to seek solace in the woods, which he felt were calling him. Silvester lives in a small town with an extensive wooded area which he described as unbelievably beautiful. Although he had moved away during the time of great loss, he felt led by nature to the woods where he now lives. Outside of his front door was the most beautiful white pine: he described it as the most beautiful pine in the city. His whole property was surrounded by ancient, magnificent trees.

At the hardest of times, experiencing the most profound loss, desperation and emotional collapse, Silvester found momentary peace in nature. He was drawn to his precious, beautiful earth for healing and an intangible sense of holistic wellbeing, even in the midst of pain and trauma.

Silvester's despair, loss and anxiety seemed unrelenting. During this time, with these feelings, he went into the woods and experienced little glimpses of hope in the beauty of nature. Silvester felt called by the woods to go out into them. He felt that they were very sacred to him. Initially Silvester did not have much energy, going outside for perhaps 10 minutes at a time. He began to do this on a daily basis. This gradually increased and Silvester now spends a lot of time out in nature to the point that he feels that he lives among the trees. These glimpses of hope were momentary feelings of connection, of feeling grounded and of a sense of oneness. Even during times of intense anxiety, depression and loneliness Silvester experienced the power of nature, taking messages that have stayed with him. He felt that he could get close to butterflies, that the deer would get close to him and that these experiences offered him a connection and a polarity and a relief from the depths of despair that he was experiencing.

Silvester had amazing 'wow' kind of moments during his time of despair – he felt intimate and connected with both polarities of his experience. Silvester was experiencing deep pain on a personal level and at the same time joy and bliss through seeing the wonder of nature and through experiencing connection. Silvester felt that nature showed him his entire experience.

Having had his life turned upside down, Silvester found solace in the most fundamental way of being. He gradually felt himself opened to an energy and healing, a little at a time. This connectedness and peacefulness contrasted with the overwhelming anxiety that he also felt, showing him a little hope in the darkest of nights. During the most difficult times he saw the beauty of nature and the magnificence of nature unfolding before him.

Silvester felt that going with the flow of the energy, particularly moving in nature, helped anxiety dissipate over time. Being in the woods seemed to be the only sense of peace and solace that he could find. He described how one beautiful day he was just sitting there and he noticed that the trees were gently blowing in the breeze and that the river was running past him and that the birds were flying. This, and other similar experiences, helped Silvester begin to find some contentment. Silvester felt that nature has taught him to be at peace with what is. From these experiences Silvester felt a sense of connectedness and peacefulness. He in his now in his 50s and feels that he has searched all his life for what he has found in nature. Silvester feels that his whole life has been impacted by his experiences and he tries to bring awareness of his relationship with nature into all aspects of how he lives. He feels that this is a process that he is constantly part of, and that nature continues to refine him.

Prior to spending extended periods of time in nature, Silvester never felt that he was grounded. Now he feels a strong sense of being grounded and embodied and that he has come to know himself and his experience at a deeper level. This gives him a sense of solace, a sense of trust in nature, a feeling of being taken care of, of being settled, rooted in nature. This is experienced as being a move from head to heart, or as if head and heart have come together. There is a deep contentment through feeling embodied in nature; that he has found who he really is through feeling more embodied. Silvester referred to the Bhagavad Gita, a very rich spiritual text, and the struggle that Arjuna had to bring his heart and his mind together. It is this sense of oneness, this merging together, that Silvester describes experiencing in nature.

Silvester experienced a physical renewal being in nature, particularly when he moved to live among the woods. Recently Silvester was sitting outside and felt that he was being sustained by nature. Part of this feeling is a sense of physical connection, of his body being made of and in nature. This is also reflected in nature providing alternative cures to his ailments, which he feels nature helped him navigate. Silvester experienced a sense of communing with nature and of being at one. He would look at a flower and just lay there on the path, and stare at and feel a sense of communion with this flower. People would walk by him and, he supposed, think that he was crazy. One day he was standing there in front of a tree and he felt that he could feel the tree breathing him in and him breathing the tree in, and experienced a sense of oneness. These very powerful experiences of connection started to become more routine for him. Slowly nature helped Silvester move a little towards accepting his experiences. Focusing on the present provided a momentary relief from the trauma that had happened and opened his heart to wonder and awe.

Silvester views nature as a sacred mother that has given him life. He feels that he has a similar relationship with nature as he did with his birth mother. Something about his experience of being in nature feels like being cradled or held. Silvester experiences being in touch with what he calls the 'divine feminine' in nature, which is where he feels that he moves and communicates more from his heart rather than from cognitive or intellectual understanding.

Silvester feels that there is an infinite source in nature that is indescribable. Within that single creation there is infinite variety that Silvester finds deeply awe inspiring. Nothing is repeated, everything is born, lives and dies uniquely and yet as part of one universal existence. Silvester experiences a divine leading and divinely inspired guide that comes from nature and he experiences being called by this spirit of nature. He feels that the divine is in everything – this is something that he used to believe on an intellectual level and that he has now experienced very personally.

Silvester feels that when he is in nature he is talking to the earth and asking for guidance about how to hear nature's wisdom. Silvester feels that there is a part of him that is very much up in the clouds, the skies, and that is connected in another worldly way, rather than just at a physical level.

What matters?

When we consider the boundaries of our lives, in the context of our place in the wider world, our perspective is encouraged to shift from what can be rather self-important illusions of being the centre of everything (Deurzen 2012). Indeed Bateson's (1972) articulation of the cybernetic epistemology suggests that the individual mind is not solely located in the body; that the mind on a personal level is merely a sub-system where the larger Mind is comparable to what we call God. Bateman's writing suggests that this larger structure is perhaps what people understand as God and that 'it is still immanent in the total inter-connected social system and planetary ecology' (Bateson 1972, p. 467).

Nature and metaphor

It is not just being in wild nature that has the power to transform; metaphors from nature are taken into daily life and provide reassurance and sustenance. For example, a friend of mine described the healing power of watching the snow blow away in the wind in the mountains and how this provided a beautiful metaphor at a relative's cremation: a reminder of the momentum of life and death in nature and being part of a wider, universal system. Life's boundaries and limitations are experienced in nature's processes and seasons, weathering storms internally and externally, realizing the limitations of control over what life throws as us and gaining alterative perspectives. Exercise 8.1 helps facilitate insight into potential distress through the use of nature's metaphors.

Exercise 8.1 Seasonal wheels

Seasonality and weather are two aspects of nature that seem to provide important metaphors for emotional experience. Working with these metaphors provides valuable insight into a person's struggles, attitudes and present focus. Use the diagram to explore and note ideas emerging from the questions that follow.

- Where do you, or your client or supervisee, see themselves in this cycle?

- What attitude do you have or do they have towards the cycle?

- Do you or they feel that the cycle is happening too quickly, or perhaps too slowly?

- How does it feel to be part of this larger picture – to be part of these wider, universal forces that are outside of our individual levels of control?

Add words around the outer edges of the circles that best describe the felt experience and meaning of the seasons.

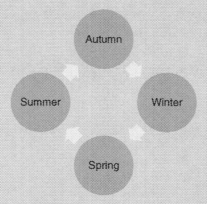

Meaning: A heuristic exploration

To re-connect us or our clients with the potential of our connection in nature, particularly spiritually, we need to consider how it might have mattered previously. Exercise 8.2 in nature can be undertaken in pairs or individually as a reflective exercise.

Exercise 8.2 A heuristic exploration of meaning in nature

Begin by trying to remember a particular powerful or meaningful experience that you have had in nature. It does not matter whether this is a recent experience or happened a long time ago, or whether it is a moment that you have explored previously or not. Consider the following questions:

- Briefly describe the context of your experience

- Where were you? What were you doing?

- What was the experience like emotionally?

- What were you feeling emotionally?

- What meaning or sense do you make of the experience?

- Has this impacted on your life since?

- What qualities of this experience stand out for you?

- What is it like talking about it now?

Use these guide or prompt questions to really explore the detail of your experience. Encourage yourself, or the other person, to be as open as possible. Try to put to one side everyday assumptions related to what is right, sensible or rational.

The detail of transformative experiences in nature – the spiritual dimension

In my research on transformative experiences in nature there were key themes that emerged that were particularly related to the spiritual dimension (Macgregor 2013). Perhaps these emerged precisely because they are outside of our normal discourse, and therefore providing an opportunity to bring them to light is more important and unusual. Beginning with a loss of self, people also described feeling part of something greater, not being alone, shifting perspective and feeling that their souls were nourished.

Being in nature transforms what is experienced as negative in day-to-day life into something much more manageable. It is much harder to get cross about minor irritations and insignificant matters in nature; being in nature shifts what is important. Focus on detail is also lessened; there is a feeling of stepping back to obtain a broader perspective. Social ideas of what is important are still present during the experience, but they take on less significance and seem more inconsequential. There is a strong understanding of the arbitrary nature of many of the rules by which life is led. This leads to a greater clarity about what matters and what is relevant. These, and other significant experiences, are expanded on in the rest of this chapter.

From 'doing and observing' towards 'being'

In nature, there is a gradual shift in perspective from doing and observing towards a focus on being. Everyday self-judgements that are based on social constructs are not experienced as meaning quite so much, partly as a result of experiencing an increase in self-acceptance and through a greater awareness of being embodied.

People's perspective is expanded through appreciation of the vastness and infinite diversity of nature, and this tends to encourage moving away from thinking too narrowly and questioning more usual stereotypes of what is and is not acceptable. Through observing a range of other diverse beings in nature living their own lives there is a revising of perspective of self to appreciate uniqueness rather than to fall into the measurement parameters of competitive conformity.

As well as some areas of life retreating in importance, some areas increase in focus. Throughout the eco-therapy literature and in my research findings there are examples of an increased value of focusing on the detail of present experience: the heron building its nest, the snowflake as it falls, the rhythmic sound of rain hitting tarpaulin.

Experiencing loss of self

On some occasions, transformative experience involves experiencing a loss of self as part of a growing feeling of strong interconnection. The feeling of merging or being at one in nature is likened to losing one self, or to a sort of death, as the feeling of being part of something greater is born. While this feeling of strong interconnection and losing a sense of defined self sometimes feels spiritual, at the same time it is tinged with a sadness, described as a letting go of a sense of ego in order to experience being at one with nature. There is a distinctly spiritual quality to this as boundaries of self are experienced more fluidly through the experience of being a part of nature. It is also connected to relational acceptance and through being very aware of and focused on the present. The acceptance of present relational experience is part of the letting go of self because it places less value on a social construction of self – who one thinks one is – and more on the actual experiencing.

Part of the experience is an awareness in nature that the experience of self is environmentally dependent, rather than a standalone isolated entity.

Being part of a system: connection and isolation

Nature shows hints of experience, a picture of the world that is experienced as equally applicable to self, since self and world are appreciated as part of the same system. Nature is turned to for guidance as if nature holds a mirror to self-experience. Awareness of being part of nature feels liberating, since it limits the power of each individual and the consequence of each choice.

Contemplating the vastness of the system and realizing the limited impact of each moment of experience provides a context that is reassuring. The small stuff really is not the end of the world. At the same time, in the midst of feeling connected to nature there is a sense of being in touch with the truth of being ultimately alone and of our individual isolation, in that each being passes in its own time, place and space. Each person has their individual and unique boundaries within the whole, and makes their own individual meaning in their own life.

Not being alone

The awareness of not being alone in nature gives a sense of belonging and security even at times where we might feel isolated from our fellow human beings. There is a notable distinction between being isolated from other people and feeling lonely: nature may be sensed at times as if it is an 'other', as if the earth speaks to us and guides us. Part of connecting with nature in this way also shows something of the connections with other people, since we are all part of the same whole. This brings a different slant to the more usual separate view of individuals existing as isolated entities that we discussed in early chapters. On occasions nature is described as a friend, with different facets of nature being personified in descriptions of transformative experience. At times, not being in nature but observing it can feel painful, a noticeable experiential separation. Connection with nature is yearned for.

The experience of self being connected relates to historical connection, connecting in some sense through the land to ancestors. This has been my enduring, reassuring perspective on many walking trips in the Welsh mountains. I walk in the footsteps of my grandparents and connect with their love and my ancestry as I traverse the landscape. Being in nature is also described as being part of a biological heritage. Feeling re-connection with the earth and land grounds the self in a more enduring context.

Beyond the self

At times the feeling of loss of sense of self in nature is experienced as being at one with the trees, rocks or grass. As I walk through the mists of the mountainside, I lose a sense of where the boundaries of 'I' stop and the clouds around me begin. This feeling of being part of a greater, vast whole is often difficult to quantify and detail. For me and for many others, this interconnection feels deeply spiritual, linked to something that seems far greater, beyond self that is difficult to articulate and that, at least for me, does not require intellectual understanding. It has been likened by others to Buddhist

Nirvana and has also been described as being like a faith: 'Hosannah! Not in the highest, but right here, right now, this!' (Goodenough 1998, p. 169).

In Chapter 6 we appreciated how being in nature has the potential to question our boundaries of self and to challenge fixed ideas of who we are. From a spiritual perspective, being in nature has the potential to allow us to experience connection beyond that which we understand. This sense of expansion is part of a recurrent theme of going beyond or expanding a fixed idea of self – perhaps connecting with or pointing to something beyond cognitive understanding. At least in part, faith and religions are based on trusting that there is sense to be made of that which eludes our understanding. People around the world regularly and routinely put their trust in something outside of the limitations of their own experience.

The feminine spirit

Transformation in nature can sometimes feel like returning to earlier states of innocence, being held and nurtured by mother nature, a spiritual, other-worldly experience. Being in touch with the 'divine feminine' in nature is a description for connecting with a wider, more heartfelt understanding than the intellectual; one that feels more like an intuitive consciousness.

An unreal experience

In powerful moments of transformation there is a surreal or unreal feeling, a sense of magic and awe outside of everyday experience and difficult to pinpoint or capture. Part of this is described as feeling as if in heaven and feeling out of body. Time seems suspended and there is an ethereal, intensely peaceful moment. The experience seems to be full of wonder and profoundly moving, impacting on life after the moment, as if nothing feels quite the same – as if a different part of reality and life has been glimpsed that opens up awareness across all parts of life.

The infinite unseen

What is not seen in nature provides a sense of connection with something greater and a vastness that is described as feeling spiritual as well as being associated with the unconscious. Looking below the surface into the depths or beyond the stars for energy, inspiration and motivation is sometimes experienced as being as important as being aware of what is seen in nature. There is a spiritual feeling of being in nature as a result of the awareness of both the tiny detail and how each part links into the vastness of the overall system. The awareness of the infinite provides a reassuring peace, at the same time as creating an urgency to make each moment have meaning as part of the bigger picture. As well as the awe-inspiring feeling there is also an awareness that nothing is repeated within nature's creation. Nature is experienced as being divine and there is a feeling of it being worshipped and personified that takes on a religious quality.

Being in awe-inspiring nature can sometimes have a quality akin to that of worshipping the unknown: 'The mysterious lawfulness of the universe – material, relational, personal and ontological – is enough to fill the human heart with a sense of marvel, awe and exuberance' (Maslow 1970, p. 127). Returning to Maslow's exploration of peak experiences reminds us that the sorts of experiences that we might previously have thought of as only within the reach of prophets or at the heart of religion are in fact potentially transcendental experiences open to us all (Maslow 1970).

Implications for practice

1. Being in nature has the potential for deep spiritual experiences that are sometimes difficult to put into words. At the same time, it can help us and our clients to value that which is wordless and accept that we cannot always make sense of things.

2. The physical dimension and the spiritual dimension are all part of holistic experience: too often the spiritual dimension is approached as if it is disconnected and ethereal, split off from the earth.

3. Human beings need peak experiences and life is pretty dull without the sorts of experiences that Maslow described. Even in our rushed, busy lives it is worth encouraging clients (and ourselves) to consider how they might make time and space for widening their daily life to include potential peak moments.

4. When working with clients who describe feeling depressed, take time to assess their relationship with nature and to explore what matters to them.

5. Help clients to explore their experiences as holistically as possible, making room for sensory and spiritual exploration as much as for emotional and cognitive understanding.

9

Natural Integration

To some extent we are always in nature, in that we are living, breathing beings dependent on the sustenance of our planet. Having a greater awareness of and more focused relationship with our natural world can reap huge benefits for us, the other inhabitants of our world and our environment. Appreciating our being in nature is important.

When we connect wholly in nature we have the potential for it to sustain us, inspire us, evoke wonder, help us feel connected, expand our awareness and provide emotional healing. Whether we have a 'lightbulb' moment of powerful transformative experiences or a more gradual feeling of awakening or connection, focusing on the relationship impacts in an enduring way on our lives. We are deeply reinvigorated. Our everyday routines, perspectives and meanings are shifted and shaken up.

Place matters

The *place* of our existence is central to our experience. We have emotional and historical connections to places. In contrast to how we often view much of the location of our experience, place is important both in facilitating emotional awareness and to the experience and meaning of self.

Being in nature helps us re-connect with our personal, internal rhythms, and facilitates bodily relaxation. In a world in which the mental and intellectual is privileged over the physical, re-connecting with our experience of being embodied (while putting aside judgement and social ideas about what this means) enables us to trust in our being as a locus of evaluation. When we are in tune with nature (and our being in nature) we shift to a more present focus. Part of what it is to be human is to face pain, heartache and loss and live with anxiety. As cognitive, reflective beings it is easy and natural for us to ruminate on such experiences, particularly when they are enduring and chronic. Being in nature seems to shift us to focus a little more on being in the present; particularly important at very difficult times when we might feel trapped or overwhelmed by worries about the future or be trying to come to terms with past events. In much of therapy there is an assumption that talking about experience is fruitful in an attempt to heal psychological and emotional pain; yet, there are times when words do not make sense, when facilitating acceptance and peace is what we need. Sometimes the most powerful healing comes from accepting that there will be parts of life that do not seem fair, that make no intellectual, causal sense, that affront our sense of what is right or just. Determined forays into nature help us accept the universe, and our troubled part in it, just as it is. In the same way that it is impossible for most of us to truly understand the scale of our galaxy, or how our planet and species came into existence in the first place, acknowledging that sometimes things 'just are' is just as valuable as making sense of it. This provides a small, yet important rebalancing in a mental health culture that is biased firmly towards understanding, talking things through, curing, changing, and symptom alleviation.

Our place, the universe

The relationship between the individual and their place in the greater system is an important realization that tends to *arise* out of significant moments in nature. We become aware perhaps of just how out of touch we are with what is already in the world: a recurring part of rediscovering a connection. We approach life less analytically in nature and our self-awareness begins to seem more embodied and more authentic: a 'bodily knowledge' arising from our experience rather than being imposed by ideas of who we, or other people, want us to be. Throughout the eco-therapy literature and in my research, nature seems to help uncover feelings and experiences that might previously have been hidden and there is a markedly different quality to emotional experiences – again something that we find hard to capture and put into words. While there is a feeling of knowing oneself in feeling connected and part of nature there is also a feeling of loss of self, losing a sense of being strongly defined and of being self-conscious. Day-to-day niggles seem much more manageable when considered in the context of the vastness of the system.

Our perspectives are widened through the beginnings of an appreciation of the vastness of nature, and this in turn encourages us not to think too narrowly and to avoid stereotyping ourselves as we accept the appreciation of the infinite difference and diversity in nature. Through observing the myriad other species on our planet living their own lives we can move towards a revision of our perspective of self and increase our appreciation of uniqueness rather than striving towards competitive conformity.

At times, being in nature is deeply spiritual. Powerful transformative moments feel like returning to a state of innocence, to experiences either beyond or before words. Such transformative moments are humbling, full of wonder and awe and difficult to quantify, moving beyond self and intellectual understanding.

The self–nature relationship: Implications for therapy

The self–nature relationship is more overtly focused on in eco-therapy and eco-psychology than in other therapy practice, where it is virtually ignored. The eco-therapy and eco-psychology approaches place this relationship as central to therapy, and suggest that there is something broken or destructive in the relationship that, if healed, would lead to increased wellbeing and healing: the self–nature relationship is the exclusive therapeutic focus and backdrop. In my findings I found it almost impossible to extract any understanding on one facet of existence, such as the physical dimension, without it being correlated to transformation or change across the other levels (Macgregor 2013). We do ourselves, and our planet, a disservice when we attempt to see one part of the picture without a firm, considered acknowledgement of the whole vista.

Practitioners of all theoretical persuasions are urged to consider how to include nature in practice so that expanded awareness and implications for meaning are brought into therapeutic endeavours with our clients. There is no need or justification to ignore this relationship. We should try not to leave out physical wellbeing from mental or emotional health discussions; neither should we extract the beings that we are from our natural, biological and environmental context.

While this might point towards incorporating therapeutic work outside in nature, it also equally leans towards rebalancing the focus on the dimensions in indoor psychotherapy practice so that at the very least 'place' becomes an important part of phenomenological exploration of experience. Bringing consideration of the 'where' more overtly into therapy, perhaps by reflecting on questions such as 'what place might feel right for you?' or 'how was that felt in that place?' might begin to address this. At the moment, the locus of distress or wellbeing is often explored on the personal, social or spiritual dimensions but rarely in relation to place.

Place as the centre of experience: Implications for therapy

Place is a central part of our lived experience, rather than a static location in which we exist, and this urges us to reconsider how we perceive and approach place in psychotherapy. If it follows that place is central to experience in nature then consideration is needed in psychotherapy of how being in particular nature helps particular emotional experiences for particular people. As well as helping our clients think about their experiences in and relationship with nature we also need to encourage exploration of their relationship in what we might loosely term 'non-natural' environments. This is not to try and reach a conclusion that suggests that being in one particular environment is correlated with a particular sense or feeling; rather it is to acknowledge that part of the experience of being *is* place and that *where* we are might matter as much as who we are with. Present psychotherapy practice places limited focus on this aspect of the physical dimension, in my experience at least. For example, in routine initial assessment forms any physical dimension questions tend to relate to the body or health. Exploring with our clients the 'where' of their experience along with the 'who' and 'how' potentially opens up a different kind of exploration and awareness.

The physical and spiritual dimensions are deeply inter-twined and this raises questions again for the 'status' of nature and place, the physical dimension, in therapy writing and practice. Often place is relegated to a sort of two-dimensional platform on which life occurs, rather than being an integral part of its creation, worthy of critical investigation.

Implications for emotional and self-awareness

People may experience an embodied awareness liberated from words or understandings when they are in nature. This stands in contrast to some of the assumptions of therapy practice, particularly that verbal and cognitive understanding is facilitative and emotionally helpful. Much of therapy practice rests on an assumption that putting into words previously unarticulated experience is helpful and a worthy cause, whereas much of the eco-therapy literature and my own research suggest that emotional healing can arise through liberation from having to make sense of and articulate experience. Part of the emotional transformation in nature experience rests on connecting to non-verbal experience without any need to make it verbal. This might also raise possibilities for the therapeutic potential of being in nature with people that have language or communication difficulties.

A final reflection on emotional experiences in nature: if emotions are experienced differently in nature, and feelings are experienced as being freer and more embodied in nature, then conducting therapy inside might actually put barriers or constraints on the emotional experience in therapy.

Ideas for practitioner awareness and therapy training

An existential approach is focused on considering the self-in-relation. Although most commonly the 'in-relation' refers to another being of some sort, existential practice is ideally placed to bring 'nature' and 'place', more routinely into the 'in-relation' than is usual in mainstream training and practice of psychotherapy and counselling (I was hugely encouraged by my supervisors, Rosemary Lodge and Emmy van Deurzen to conduct my doctoral research on this relationship, so there are enlightened academics and training institutions not in the eco-therapy or eco-psychology fields that are less narrowly focused than others, but a quick scour of the top syllabus of most of the doctoral and masters-level training programmes shows very little coverage at all of the natural world and our relationship to it).

Research suggests that the person of the counsellor and the quality and emotional connection in the therapeutic relationship is central to therapeutic healing. If we consider self-awareness in isolation from place we ignore an important quality of relational experience. If we focus on self or other awareness without reference to place, we might be limiting who we think we are and how we are available to others. Expanding the quality and texture of where we train and practise might be correlated with expanding the potential quality and texture of our therapeutic relationships, enriching the whole experience for us and for our clients.

References

Abram, D. (1996). *The Spell of the Sensuous: Perception and Language in a More-than Human World.* New York: Pantheon Books.

Action on Addiction UK (2017). https://www.actiononaddiction.org.uk/treating-the-wider-effects, accessed 10 September 2018.

Alive (2017). http://www.alive.org.au/self-harm/, accessed 23 October 2017.

American Psychiatric Association (APA) (2013). *Diagnostic and Statistical Manual of Mental Disorders Fourth Edition Text Revision (DSM-V).* Arlington, TX: American Psychiatric Association (APA).

Bateson, G. (1972). *Steps to an Ecology of Mind.* London: Chicago Press.

Berger, R. and McLeod (2006). 'Incorporating Nature into Therapy: A Framework for Practice'. *Journal of Systemic Therapies*, 25(2), 80–94.

Beringer, A. (2004). 'Toward an Ecological Paradigm in Adventure Programming'. *Journal of Experiential Education*, 27(1), 51–66 (London: Sage).

Bliss, S. (2009). In L. Buzzell and C. Chalquist (Eds), *Ecotherapy Healing with Nature in Mind.* San Francisco, CA: Sierra Books.

Bodnar, S. (2012). '"It's Snowing Less": Narratives of a Transformed Relationship Between Humans and Their Environments'. In M.-J. Rust and N. Totton (Eds), *Vital Signs: Psychological Responses to Ecological Crisis.* London: Karnac Books.

Brazier, C. (2011). *Acorns Among the Grass: Adventures in Ecotherapy.* Alresford: O Books.

Brown, C. and Toadvine, T. (2003). *Eco-Phenomenology Back to the Earth Itself.* Albany, NY: Suny Press.

Buber, M. (1937). *I and Thou.* London: Continuum.

Buzzell, L. and Chalquist, C. (2009). *Ecotherapy: Healing with Nature in Mind.* San Francisco: Sierra Club Books.

Camus, A. (1968). *Lyrical and Critical Essays.* New York: Knopf.

Clinebell, H. (1996). *Ecotherapy Healing Ourselves Healing the Earth.* Norristown, PA: Augsburg Fortress.

Cohn, H. (1997). *Existential Thought and Therapeutic Practice.* London: Sage.

Conrad, J. (1900). *Lord Jim.* Kindle Edition. Public Domain Books: Retrieved from Amazon.com (2006).

Cooper, M. (2003). *Existential Therapies*. London: Sage.

Counselling Psychology Review (CPR). (2008). 'Counselling Psychology and the Natural World', 23(2). Leicester: British Psychological Society.

Csikszentmihalyi, M. (1990). *Flow: The Psychology of Optimal Experience*. New York: Harper and Row.

De Young, R. (2010). 'Restoring Mental Vitality in an Endangered World: Reflections on the Benefits of Walking'. *Ecopsychology*, 2(1), 13–22.

Deurzen, E. van (2008). 'Vox-Pop'. *Counselling Psychology Review*, 23(2), 53–54.

Deurzen, E. van (2009). *Everyday Mysteries – Existential Dimensions of Psychotherapy*. London: Routledge.

Deurzen, E. van (2012). *Existential Counselling and Psychotherapy in Practice*, Third Edition. London: Sage.

Deurzen, E. van and Adams, M. (2016). *Skills in Existential Counselling and Psychotherapy*. London: Sage.

Deurzen, E. van and Arnold-Baker, C. (2005). *Existential Perspectives on Human Issues*. Basingstoke: Palgrave Macmillan.

Donne, J. (1623). 'Devotions Upon Emergent Occasions'. Meditation #17 http://www.online-literature.com/donne/409/, accessed 10 May 2018.

Donne, J. (2012). *The Best of John Donne*. North Charleston, SC: CreateSpace.

Dwivedi, K.N. and Harper, P.B. (2004). 'Promoting the Emotional Well-being of Children and Adolescents and Preventing Their Mental Ill Health'. *Mental Health Review Journal*, 10, 4–14 (London: Jessica Kingsley Publishers).

Emerson, R. (1849). *Nature*. Boston, MA and Cambridge: James Munroe.

Fisher, A. (2002). *Radical Ecopsychology: Psychology in the Service of Life*. New York: State University of New York Press.

Foster, S. and Little, M. (1987). *The Book of the Visionquest: Personal Transformation in the Wilderness*. New York: Prentice Hall Press.

Foster, S. and Little, M. (1999). *The Four Shields: The Initiatory Seasons of Human Nature*. Big Pine, CA: Lost Borders Press.

Gibran, K. (1926/1991). *The Prophet*. London: Pan Macmillan.

Goodenough, U. (1998). *The Sacred Depths of Nature*. New York: Oxford University Press.

Greenway, R. (1995). 'The Wilderness Effect and Ecopsychology'. In T. Roszak, M.E. Gomes and A.D. Kanner (Eds), *Ecopsychology: Restoring the Earth, Healing the Mind*. San Francisco: Sierra Club Books.

Greenwood, M., and Leeuw, S.D. (2007). 'Teachings from the Land: Indigenous People, Our Health, Our Land, and Our Children'. *Canadian*

Journal of Native Education, 30(1), 48–53, 189. https://www.researchgate.net/publication/313821932, accessed 10 September 2018.

Harper, S. (1995). 'The Way of Wilderness'. In T. Roszak, M.E. Gomes and A.D. Kanner (Eds), *Ecopsychology: Restoring the Earth, Healing the Mind*. San Francisco: Sierra Club Books.

Heidegger, M. (1927). *Being and Time* (Trans. J. Macquarrie and E.S. Robinson). New York: Harper & Row, 1962.

Heidegger, M. (2010). *Country Path Conversations* (Trans. B.W. Davis). Bloomington, IN: Indiana University Press.

Hicks, C. (2008). 'Vox-Pop'. *Counselling Psychology Review*, 23(2), 7–8.

Higley, N. and Milton, M. (2008). 'Our Connection to the Earth – A Neglected Relationship in Counselling Psychology?' *Counselling Psychology Review*, 23(2), 10–23.

Hillman, J. (1995). 'A Psyche the Size of the Earth'. In T. Roszak, M.E. Gomes and A.D. Kanner (Eds), *Ecopsychology: Restoring the Earth, Healing the Mind*. San Francisco: Sierra Club Books.

Hippocrates (2009 [nd]). *On Airs, Waters and Places*. Gloucester: Dodo Press.

Hoffman, E. (1998). 'Peak Experiences in Childhood: An Exploratory Study'. *Journal of Humanistic Psychology*, 38(1), 109–120.

International Community for Ecopsychology (ICE) (2011). https://www.ecopsychology.org, accessed 10 September 2018.

Jordan, M. (2009a). *Therapy Today: 4*. Lutterworth: BACP.

Jordan, M. (2009b). 'Nature and Self: An Ambivalent Attachment?' *Ecopsychology*, 1(1), 26–31. http://eprints.brighton.ac.uk/10766/1/Martin_Jordan_nature_and_self_eco.2008.pdf, accessed 10 September 2018.

Jordan, M. (2014). *Nature and Therapy. Understanding Counselling and Psychotherapy in Outdoor Spaces*. London: Routledge.

Jordan, M. and Marshall, H. (2010). 'Taking Counselling and Psychotherapy Outside: Destruction or Enrichment of the Therapeutic Frame?' *European Journal of Psychotherapy Counselling*, 12(4), 345–359.

Jordan, M. and Hinds, J. (2016). *Ecotherapy Theory, Research and Practice*. London: Palgrave.

Jung, C. (1967). *Memoires, Dreams, Reflections*. London: Fontana.

Jung, C. (1969). *The Structure and Dynamics of the Psyche*. Princeton, NJ: Princeton University Press.

Jung, C. (1975 vol I and II). *C.G. Jung Letters I and II* (Ed. G. Adler). Princeton, NJ: Princeton University Press.

Kanner, M.E. and Gomes, M.E. (1995). 'The All-Consuming Self'. In T. Roszak, M.E. Gomes and A.D. Kanner (Eds), *Ecopsychology: Restoring the Earth, Healing the Mind*. San Francisco: Sierra Club Books.

Kaplan, R. and Kaplan, S. (1989). *The Experience of Nature: A Psychological Perspective*. Cambridge: Cambridge University Press.

Key, D. (2003). 'The Ecology of Adventure'. Unpublished, Centre for Human Ecology, Edinburgh.

Kierkegaard, S. (1844/2014). *The Concept of Anxiety* (Trans. A. Hannay). New York: Norton.

Laing, R.D. (1960). *The Divided Self*. London: Penguin Books.

Levine, D. (1994). 'Breaking Through Barriers : Wilderness Therapy for Sexual Assault Survivors'. *Women and Therapy*, 15(3–4), 175–184 (Special Issue : Wilderness therapy for women: the power of adventure).

Linden, S. and Grut, J. (2002) *The Healing Fields*. London: Frances Lincoln.

Luther Standing Bear. http://www.greatthoughtstreasury.com/author/luther-standing-bear-aka-ota-kte-or-mochunozhin, accessed 8 May 2018.

Macgregor, C. (2013). 'The Nature of Existence'. Unpublished, available Middlesex University.

Macy, J. and Brown, M.Y. (1998). *Coming Back to Life: Practices to Reconnect our Lives, Our World*. Gabriola Island: New Society Publishers.

Maiteny, P. (2012). 'Longing to be Human: Evolving Ourselves in Healing the Earth'. In M.-J. Rust and N. Totton (Eds), *Vital Signs: Psychological Responses to Ecological Crisis*. London: Karnac Books.

Maslow, A.H. (1970). *Religions, Values and Peak Experiences*. New York: Penguin.

Mental Health Foundation (2017). https://www.mentalhealth.org.uk/a-to-z/s/self-harm, accessed 25 October 2017.

Merleau-Ponty, M. (1962). *The Phenomenology of Perception*. London: Routledge.

Merleau-Ponty, M. (1969). *The Visible and the Invisible*. Evanston, IL: Northwestern University Press.

Messer-Diehl, E.R. (2009). 'Gardens that Heal'. In L. Buzzell and C. Chalquist (Eds), *Ecotherapy: Healing with Nature in Mind*. San Francisco: Sierra Club Books.

Metzner, R. (1999). *Green Psychology: Transforming Our Relationship to the Earth*. Rochester, NY: Park Street Press.

Milton, M. (2008). 'Wisdom from the Wilderness'. *Counselling Psychology Review*, 23(2), 36–46.

Milton, M. (2010). *Therapy and Beyond: Counselling Psychology Contributions to Therapeutic and Social Issues*. Chichester: Wiley.

Mind (2007). *Ecotherapy the Green Agenda for Mental Health*. London: Mind Publications.

Mind (2011). 'About EcoMinds'. http://www.mind.org.uk/ecominds, accessed 1 April 2011.

Mind (2017). http://www.mind.org.uk/information-support/types-of-mental-health-problems/sleep-problems/, accessed 10 April 2018.

Minkowski, E. (1933/1970). *Lived Time: Phenomenological and Psychopathological Studies* (Trans. N. Mekel). Evanston, IL: Northwestern University Press.

Native American Indians (2011). http://native-americans-online.com/native-american-vision-quest.html, accessed 1 August, 2017.

Orbach, S. (2000). *The Impossibility of Sex: Stories of the Intimate Relationship Between Therapist and Patient*. New York: Touchstone.

Perraton Mountford, C. (2006). 'Open-Centred Ecosophy: Or How to Do Environmentally Interesting Things with Dr. Rogers' Therapeutic Conditions'. In J. Moore and C. Purton (Eds), *Spirituality and Counselling*. Ross-on-Wye: PCCS Books.

Pienaar, M. (2011). 'An Eco-Existential Understanding of Time and Psychological Defenses: Threats to the Environment and Implications for Psychotherapy'. *Ecopsychology*, 3(1), 25–39.

Roads, M.J. (1985). *Talking with Nature, Journey into Nature*. Novato: HJ Kramer.

Rogers, C. (1951). *Client-Centered Therapy*. London: Constable.

Rogers, C. (1969). 'Towards a More Human Science of the Person'. *Journal of Humanistic Psychology*, 25(4), 7–24.

Rogers, C. (1978). 'The Formative Tendency'. *Journal of Humanistic Psychology*, 18(1), 23–26 (London: Association for Humanistic Psychology, Sage).

Roszak, T. (2001). *The Voice of the Earth*. Grand Rapids: Phanes.

Roszak, T., Gomes, M.E. and Kanner, A.D. (1995). *Ecopsychology: Restoring the Earth, Healing the Mind*. San Francisco: Sierra Club books.

Russell, K. (2001). 'What is Wilderness Therapy?' *Journal of Experiential Education*, 23(3), 70–79.

Rust, M.-J. (2008). 'Nature Hunger: Eating Problems and Consuming the Earth?' *Counselling Psychology Review*, 23(2), 70–78.

Rust, M.-J. (2009). 'Why and How Do Therapists Become Ecotherapists?' In L. Buzzell and C. Chalquist (Eds), *Ecotherapy: Healing with Nature in Mind*. San Francisco: Sierra Club Books.

Rust, M.-J. and Totton, N. (2012). *Vital Signs: Psychological Responses to Ecological Crisis*. London: Karnac Books.

Sartre, J.-P. (1946). *Existentialism and Humanism*. London: Methuen.

Sartre, J.-P (2003). *Being and Nothingness: An Essay in Phenomenological Ontology*. Abingdon: Routledge.

Sleep Council (2011). Toxic Sleep Survey https://sleepcouncil.org.uk/latest-news/toxic-sleep-the-silent-epidemic/, accessed 10 September 2018.

Snyder, J. (1989). 'The Experience of Feeling Really Connected to Nature'. *Dissertation Abstracts International*, 49, 4025-B.

Söderback, I., Söderström, M. and Schälander, E. (2004). 'Horticultural Therapy: The "Healing Garden in Rehabilitation Measures at Danderyd Hospital Rehabilitation Clinic, Sweden"'. *Pediatric Rehabilitation*, 7(4), 245–260 (London: Taylor and Francis).

Spinelli, E. (2007). *Practising Existential Psychotherapy: The Relational World*. London: Sage.

Stevens, P. (2010). 'Embedment in the Environment: A New Paradigm for Well-Being?' *Perspectives in Public Health*, 130(6), 265–269. Retrieved from http://eprints.bournemouth.ac.uk/15879/1/.

Sustainable Development Commission (2008). 'Health Place and Nature How Outdoor Environments Influence Health and Well-Being: A Knowledge Base'. Retrieved from https://research-repository.st-andrews.ac.uk/handle/10023/2180, accessed 10 September 2018

The Guardian (2018). https://www.theguardian.com/news/datablog/2009/aug/18/percentage-population-living-cities, accessed 10 September 2018.

Thompson, M. (2009). 'Reviewing Ecopsychology Research: Exploring Five Databases and Considering the Future'. *Ecopsychology*, 1(1), 32–37. doi:10.1089/eco.2008.00077.

Winter, D. and Koger, S. (2010). *The Psychology of Environmental Problems: Psychology for Sustainability*. Hove: Taylor and Francis.

World Health Organization (2017). http://www.who.int/topics/obesity/en/, accessed 10 September 2018.

World Wide Fund (WWF) for Nature (2017). https://wwf.panda.org/our_work/biodiversity accessed 10 September 2018.

Index

Abram, David (1996), 10
  earth, animate, 10
addiction, 125
American Psychiatric Association, 3,
  59, 124
ancient practices, 83–84
  holistic healing, 84–85
  medicine wheel, 85–86
  Vision Quest, 84, 104
anxiety, 43–44
  disorder, 43
  living in time and anxiety, 44

Bateson, Gregory (1972), 13–14
being-in-the-world, 8, 10, 18,
  48, 50–54, 101, 114,
  134
Berger and McLeod (2006), 15
birth and death, 47
Bodnar, (2012), 14
  body, 14
  body ideal, 63–63
  changes in way of life, 14
  disconnection and manipulation,
    55–56, 61, 65–66
  embodiment, 71–72
  feeling at home, 4
  objectification, 62–63
  self-harm, 66–67
Brazier, Caroline (2011), 47
Brown, Charles and Toadvine, Ted
  (2003), 10
  eco-phenomenology, 10

Buzzell, Linda and Chalquist, Craig
  (2009), 1, 6
  challenging the status quo, 29
  healing in nature, 44
  inner deadening, 29
  nature and disconnection,
    impact of, 24

change culture, 37–38
Clinebell, Howard (1996), 79
Cohn, Hans (1997), 43
connection in nature, 3, 7, 10, 11,
  15, 24–26, 74–75, 135–146
connections exercise, 27
depression, 42
place and connection, 24–27,
  29–30
control, 50–54
Cooper, Mick (2003), 10

dasein, 8–9
depression, 41–43, 73, 88, 91
Deurzen, Emmy van and Arnold-
  Baker, Claire (2005), 2
  anxiety, 44
  natural world, relationship
    with, 10
Deurzen, Emmy van (2008), 12
Deurzen, Emmy van (2012), 6, 100
  death, 47
  depression, holistic, 41
  four dimensions, 9, 41, 58, 112
  spirituality, 125

152

Printed in the United States
By Bookmasters